Diesterwegs
Neusprachliche
Themenhefte

für die Sekundarstufe II

Herausgegeben von John Poziemski

LONDON – a city and its people

Edited and annotated
by David Beal

Why, Sir, you find no man, at all intellectual, who is willing to leave London. No, Sir, when a man is tired of London, he is tired of life; for there is in London all that life can afford.

Samuel Johnson (1777)

VERLAG MORITZ DIESTERWEG
Frankfurt am Main

The editor and publishers are grateful to the authors, publishers and others who have given permission for the use of copyright material identified in the text. It has not been possible to identify the sources of all the material used and in such cases the publishers would welcome information from copyright owners.

ISBN 3-425-04491-5

Satz: Fotosatz Otto Gutfreund, Darmstadt
Druck: Wiesbadener Graphische Betriebe GmbH, Wiesbaden
Bindung: Großbuchbinderei Adolf Hiort, Wiesbaden

Contents

LONDON THROUGH THE AGES

A city of refuge, the mansion house of liberty.
John Milton (1608–1674)

1. Roman London

When the Romans conquered Britain in the first century they saw the strategic value of the river village and increased its importance by building the first London Bridge – a wooden structure which was a superb piece of engineering. It is thought that at first a small fort roughly 200 yards square was built and used as a garrison guarding the bridge which was the main link with the invading armies. It may also have been a mint as many early Roman coins have been found in the area. At this time Londinium was not the principal Roman city in Britain – but the new lords had a set-back when Boadicea attacked the settlement and razed it to the ground. This came about as follows. When the Romans initially invaded they made a pact with Prasutagus, the husband of Boadicea, promising not to invade his lands in East Anglia and so avoid a bloody conflict with the tribe of Iceni, who were under his command. In return Prasutagus, who had his headquarters in Colchester, allowed the Romans to use it as their administrative centre, and gave help and advice where needed. Before he died he left half his fortune to Nero, hoping that this would protect his family. It did not, and after his death the Romans confiscated his palace, wealth and property,

to invade attack, enter and take control of **Boadicea** [bəʊədɪ'siːə] also spelt: Boudica and Boudicca **East Anglia** a region of England consisting of Norfolk, Suffolk, parts of Cambridgeshire and Essex **Iceni** [aɪ'siːnaɪ] **Colchester** town in Essex, the original Roman capital of Britain (Lat. Camulodunum) **Nero** Roman emperor (AD 37–68) **to confiscate** take (private property) away from someone without payment stripped and flogged his wife and raped his daughters. Queen Boadicea, a lady of great spirit, vowed that these actions should not go unavenged. She summoned up her great Iceni army and many thousands of well trained warriors marched on Colchester and St. Albans, which they destroyed completely. She then set her sights on London and this settlement met the same fate. Before she could be captured she took poison and so escaped torment by her enemies. There is a bronze statue of Boadicea in her chariot near Westminster Pier.

After this experience the Romans thought it prudent to build a wall around the river stronghold. The settlement was extended to cover about 330 acres and the wall was built out from the original fort from the lower western corner and the upper eastern corner and eventually enclosed an area about the size of Hyde Park. The eastern wall borders on to the walls of the Tower, which was built, we presume, later. There were seven main gates in those days which are remembered in street names in modern times. These were Aldgate (the oldest of all), Bishopsgate, Moorgate, Cripplegate (this had an underground passage where late travellers could pay a toll to gain entry to the City after sundown. Cripple ist derived from an old English word meaning underground), Ludgate and the London Bridge Gate – which had taken the place of the first Billingsgate.

Before the Romans became Christians it is thought that a temple dedicated to Diana was built on the site where now stands St. Paul's Cathedral. During excavations the head of Diana was found and is preserved in the Goldsmith's Hall. After the Great Fire Wren had the task of rebuilding St. Paul's and during excavations found many Roman and Saxon remains including burial urns and sacrificial vessels – but nothing to convince him that a pagan temple to Diana was once built on the spot. However he did believe most wholeheartedly that St. Paul himself had visited these islands on his many journeys and had come to consecrate the ground where he said that a church should be built bearing his name. There is no mention in the Scriptures of St. Paul visiting these islands but the legend of the settling of

to strip remove the clothes from someone **to flog** beat with a stick or whip **to rape** have sex with s.o. against his or her will **unavenged** G. ungerächt **warriors** ['wɒrɪəz] **to set one's sights on** aim for **to meet the same fate** experience the same thing **chariot** ['tʃærɪət] a two-wheeled horse-drawn vehicle used in battles and races **to presume** think something is true without knowing for certain **Diana** [daɪ'ænə] Roman goddess of the hunt and the moon **Wren** Sir Christopher Wren, architect of St. Paul's Cathedral (1632–1723) **burial urn** [ɜ:n] container used to keep the ashes of s.o. who has died **sacrificial** [sækrɪ'fɪʃəl] used when offering something to a god

Joseph of Arimathea in Glastonbury is well known. There is another story concerning Suetonius, the early Christian Roman leader, who, while in Wales killing off the Druids, learnt some Welsh words, and on his return to London named the early church built on the site of St. Paul's 'Llanden', which is Welsh for Church of Diana, and this could also be interpreted as yet another derivation of the word London.

During the Roman occupation London thrived as did all Roman communities in Britain. Temples, houses, roads, offices were built with expertise and craftsmanship far beyond the level of civilization at that time. When the Romans left, London, like all the rest, was disorganized and unready for the Saxon hordes which had been awaiting the opportunity to attack and conquer the island which they regarded as a rich prize. London was reduced to a primitive dwelling place. The Saxons were pagan and nothing was sacred. Roman sculpture, pillars, cornices and all magnificent works of art were pulled down and used as common building stone. Soon not a piece of Roman architecture survived above the ground except the London Stone set up by the Romans as a milestone measuring distances from the City. It can still be seen today above the pavement in Cannon Street.

Jean Harrowven (1983), *Origin and Tales of London Town.* Tadworth: Kaye and Ward. pp. 12–14.

Joseph of Arimathea a rich man who buried Christ and according to legend brought the Holy Grail – the vessel used at the Last Supper and which received the blood from Christ's wounds – to England and founded a Christian settlement at Glastonbury **Glastonbury** a town in Somerset, in SW England **Suetonius Paulinus** Roman governor of Britain at the time of Boadicea's revolt. When the revolt took place he was in Wales suppressing the Druids. Because his punishment of the rebellious tribes was so severe the Emperor Nero replaced him by a new governor **Druid** an ancient Celtic priest **Saxon** a Germanic people from north Germany who conquered and settled in England in the 5th century **pillar** tall upright post made of stone used to hold up a roof **cornice** ['kɔːnɪs] ornamental border at the top edge of the front of a building or pillar

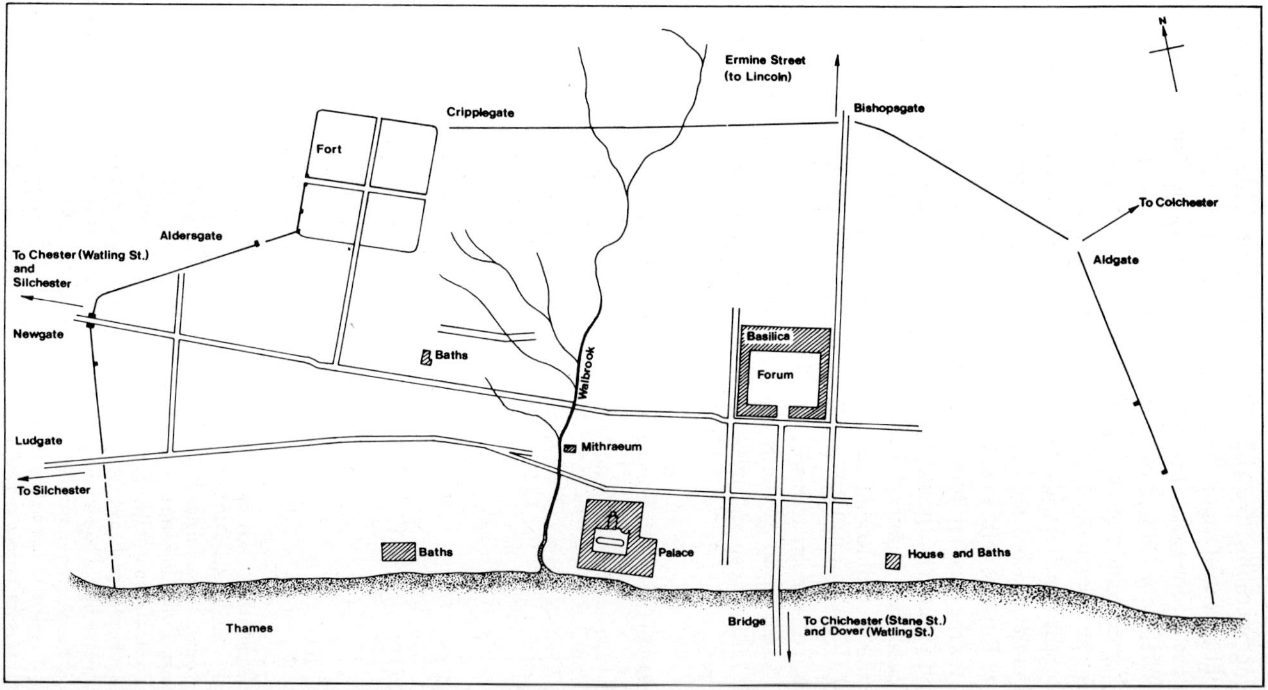

Jonathan Kiek (1984), *Everybody's Historical London*. London: Quiller Press. pp. 17–22.

Comprehension

Say which statements are *true* or *false according to the text, or if the text doesn't say.* Rewrite false statements correctly and justify your answers.

1. Before the Romans arrived in Britain the village of London did not exist.
2. The Roman village of Londinium probably had two main functions.
3. The first Roman headquarters were in Colchester.
4. The Romans attacked the Iceni and mistreated Prasutagus' family because Prasutagus left only half his fortune to Nero.
5. Boadicea and her army completely destroyed three Roman towns.
6. The Romans built a wall round London because they thought the Britons might attack it again.
7. The Roman fort was situated in the north-western corner of the Roman settlement.
8. There is no reason to think that the Romans had built a temple to Diana in London.
9. St. Paul's Cathedral got its name because St. Paul asked that a church be built in London bearing his name.
10. The Saxons drove out the Romans.
11. The reason the Saxons destroyed the Roman city of London was that they were not Christians.

Language skills

Choose a title for each paragraph and justify your choice.

Topic work

1. Discuss what factors might lead a town to be founded at a certain place and what might cause it to develop.
2. Write a short account of the early history of your own town or village, giving details of its earliest inhabitants and why it came to be founded in that particular place.

Felix Barker and Peter Jackson (1983), London: *2000 Years of a City and its People.* (*Cassell Ltd.*, London)

2. The Great Fire: An Eyewitness's Account

During the night of 2 September the Great Fire broke out. It was to rage for four days and nights, causing more damage than any similar calamity until the great blitz of 1940–2. Few lives were lost, but some four-fifths of the total area of the city was laid waste. It began accidentally in a bakehouse in Pudding Lane, but was commonly believed to have been the work of papists and the foreign enemy.

2 September. Lords Day.

Some of our maids sitting up late last night to get things ready against our feast today, Jane called us up, about 3 in the morning, to tell us of a great fire they saw in the City. So I rose, and slipped on my nightgown and went to her window, and thought it to be on the back side of Markelane at the furthest; but being unused to such fires as followed, I thought it far enough off, and so went to bed again and to sleep. About 7 rose again to dress myself, and there looked out at the window and saw the fire not so much as it was, and further off. So to my closet to set things to rights after yesterday's cleaning. By and by Jane comes and tells me that she hears that above 300 houses have been burned down tonight by the fire we saw, and that it was now burning down all Fishstreet by London Bridge. So I made myself ready presently, and walked to the Tower and there got up upon one of the high places, Sir J. Robinson's little son going up with me; and there I did see the houses at that end of the bridge all on fire, and an infinite great fire on this and the other side the end of the bridge – which, among other people, did trouble me for poor little Michell and our Sarah on the Bridge. So down, with my heart full of trouble, to the Lieutenant of the Tower, who tells me that it begun this morning in the King's bakers house in Pudding

the great blitz the bombing of London and other British cities by the German airforce during the Second World War **papist** ['peɪpɪst] (derog.) a member or supporter of the Catholic Church **against** (arch.) for **Jane** a maid **back side** (arch.) *here:* far side **Markelane** (arch.) Mark Lane **dress myself** (arch.) get dressed **not so much as it was** *here:* not as intense as it was **closet** (arch.) a small private room **above** (arch.) more than **presently** (arch.) immediately **Sir John Robinson** Lieutenant of the Tower, guardian of the Tower, appointed by the King **I did see** (arch.) I saw **Mr Michell** Pepys' father-in-law **Sarah** a servant **it begun** (arch.) it began

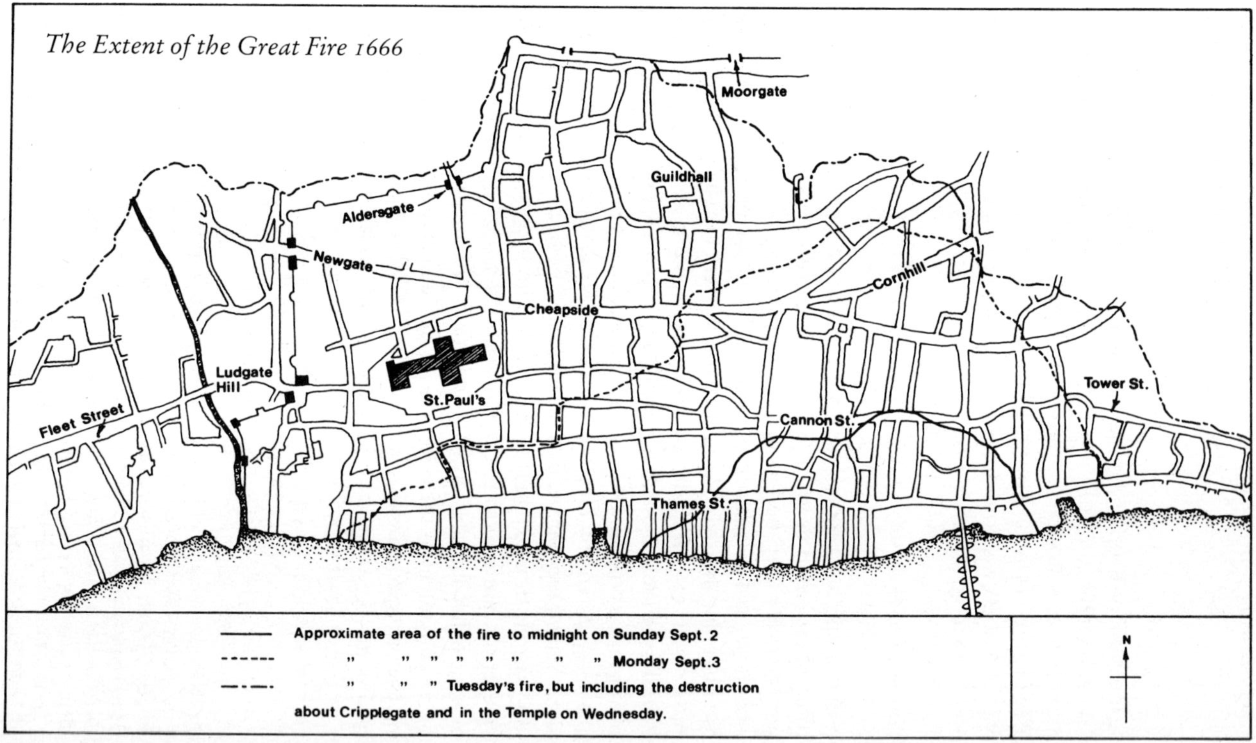

Jonathan Kiek (1984), *Everybody's Historic London*. London: Quiller Press. p. 118.

Lane, and that it hath burned down St Magnes Church and most part of Fishstreete already. So I down to the waterside and there got a boat and through bridge, and there saw a lamentable fire. Poor Michells house, as far as the Old Swan, already burned that way and the fire running further, that in a very little time it got as far as the Stillyard while I was there. Everybody endeavouring to remove their goods, and flinging into the river or bringing them into lighters that lay off. Poor people staying in their houses as long as till the very fire touched them, and then running into boats or clambering from one pair of stair by the waterside to another. And among other things, the poor pigeons I perceive were loath to leave their houses, but hovered about the windows and balconies till they were some of them burned, their wings, and fell down.

Having stayed, and in an hour's time seen the fire rage every way, and nobody to my sight endeavouring to quench it, but to remove their goods and leave all to the fire; and having seen it get as far as the Steeleyard, and the wind mighty high and driving it into the city, and everything, after so long a drought, proving combustible, even the very stones of churches. I to Whitehall with a gentleman with me who desired to go off from the Tower to see the fire in my boat – to Whitehall, and there up to the King's closet in the chapel, where people came about me and I did give them an account dismayed them all; and word was carried in to the King, so I was called for and did tell the King and Duke of York what I saw, and that unless his Majesty did command houses to be pulled down, nothing could stop the fire. They seemed much troubled, and the King commanded me to go to my Lord Mayor from him and command him to spare no houses but to pull down before the fire every way. The Duke of York bid me tell him that if he would have any more soldiers, he shall. Here meeting with Captain Cocke, I in his coach, which he lent me, and Creed with me, to Pauls; and there walked along Watling Street as well as I could, every creature coming away loaden with goods to save – and here and there sick people carried

it hath (arch.) it has **St Magnes** (arch.) St. Magnus the Martyr **Stillyard** the same as the following 'Steeleyard' **lighter** a large open flat-bottomed boat used for loading and unloading ships **drought** [draʊt] a long period without rain **combustible** able to catch fire and burn easily **Whitehall** a street leading from Trafalgar Square to the Houses of Parliament; now site of the main government offices but in Pepys' time site of Whitehall Palace, one of the King's residences; destroyed by fire in 1698 **the King** King Charles II **came about me** (arch.) gathered around me **Duke of York** James, the brother of Charles II **Lord Mayor** Sir Thomas Bludworth **bid** (arch.) asked **if he would** (arch.) if he wanted to **Captain (George) Cocke** a merchant and friend of Pepys' **John Creed** a member of the Earl of Sandwich's household and naval servant **Pauls** St Paul's Cathedral **loaden** (arch.) loaded away in beds. Extraordinary good goods carried in carts and on backs. At last met my Lord Mayor in Canning Streete, like a man spent, with a hankercher about his neck. To the King's message, he cried like a fainting woman, 'Lord, what can I do? I am spent! People will not obey me. I have been pull[ing] down houses. But the fire overtakes us faster than we can do it.' That he needed no more soldiers; and that for himself, he must go and refresh himself, having been up all night. So he left me, and I him, and walked home – seeing people all almost distracted and no manner of means used to quench the fire. The houses too, so very thick thereabouts, and full of matter for burning, as pitch and tar, in Thames Street – and warehouses of oyle and wines and brandy and other things. Here I saw Mr Isaccke Houblon, that handsome man – prettily dressed and dirty at his door at Dowgate, receiving some of his brothers things whose houses were on fire; and as he says, have been removed twice already, and he doubts (as it soon proved) that they must be in a little time removed from his house also – which was a sad consideration. And to see the churches all filling with goods, by people who themselfs should have been quietly there at this time.

Robert Latham (ed.) (1983), *The Illustrated Pepys.* London: Bell and Hyman. pp. 120–1.

spent (arch.) exhausted **hankercher** (arch.) handkerchief **about** (arch.) around **as** (arch.) like **oyle** (arch.) oil

Comprehension

Say which of the statements below are *true* or *false* according to the text or whether the text *doesn't say*.
Justify your answer by referring to the text.

1. Pepys went back to bed after seeing the fire in the middle of the night because he didn't think the fire would reach his house.
2. Pepys went to the Tower because it was a good place from which to see the fire.
3. The reason the fire was moving so fast was that nobody was trying to put it out.
4. People were not fighting the fire because they were more interested in saving their belongings.
5. Pepys went from the Tower to Whitehall by boat so that another gentleman could see the fire.
6. The King called for Pepys to tell him to order the Lord Mayor to pull down houses.
7. It was the King's proposal that houses should be pulled down to stop the fire.
8. If the Lord Mayor had wanted them he could have had soldiers to help put out the fire.
9. The Lord Mayor did not think it was a good idea to use soldiers to stop the fire.

Language skills

Complete the sentences below with one of the following words (not all the words are needed); before, after, when, since, while, during, as soon as.

1. The great fire started .... Samuel Pepys was asleep.
2. .... he had looked at the fire, he went back to bed.
3. .... he spoke to the Lieutenant of the Tower, Samuel Pepys saw the fire from the Tower.
4. .... he was in the boat, Pepys saw the fire raging through the City.
5. .... speaking to the King, Pepys went to see the Lord Mayor.
6. .... the walk along Watling Street Pepys saw people carrying their possessions away from the fire.
7. Samuel Pepys had been very busy .... 7 am.

Topic work

1. As a preparation for task 2, look for sentences containing *adjectives* and *verbs* which express Pepys' feelings and attitudes towards what he is seeing and experiencing.
2. Write a diary entry for one day in your life. Of course you will probably not have such a momentous event to report on as the Great Fire of London, but the important thing about a diary is the personal view it gives of even trivial everyday events and ordinary people. Try then to give your narrative a personal touch: what are your feelings and honest opinions of the people and incidents you report on?

3. London is a Fine Town

London is a Fine Town

O London is a dainty place,
A great and gallant city!
For all the Streets are pav'd with gold,
And all the folks are witty.
And there's your lords and ladies fine,
That ride in coach and six;
That nothing drink but claret wine,
And talk of politicks.

And there's your dames with dainty frames,
With skins as white as milk;
Dressed every day in garments gay,
Of satin and of silk.
And if your mind be so inclined
To offer them your arm,
Pull out a handsome purse of gold,
They can't resist the charm.

Street Ballad (1789)

Kenneth Baker (ed.) (1984), *London Lines*. London: Methuen. p. 20.

dainty *here:* pretty **coach and six** coach pulled by six horses **claret** ['klærət] red wine from Bordeaux **politicks** (old-fashioned spelling) **dainty** *here:* small **frames** *here:* bodies **to be inclined** G. geneigt sein

Topic work

1. What is the writer's attitude to London and its people? What gives you this impression?
2. Summarise in one sentence what the ballad is about.
3. This poem is called a ballad. This means that it was originally sung, probably to music, and might also have accompanied dance. What is it about the form of this ballad which might lead you to think it was sung? How far would you agree that this ballad 'is a kind of eighteenth century pop song'?
4. Try to write a poem about your town, in which its characteristics and those of its inhabitants are satirised.

4. The First Police Force

By the end of the eighteenth century thousands of people were making dishonest livings out of smuggling from the ships using the River Thames. Members of the Honourable West India Company took up the suggestion of an East London magistrate, Patrick Colquhoun, that a system of river patrols should be set up. With government approval they financed the project under the leadership of Colquhoun and John Harriot, working from an office based at Wapping. These Marine Police (which were formed in 1800) were the forerunners of today's Thames Division whose headquarters is still at Wapping. The 'Wet Bobs' as they came to be known were and are hard, tough men, and in the early days were recruited from the watermen or navy. Their gear included 'toe bags' – waterproof sacks which kept them warm and dry up to the waist. The practice of smuggling was greatly reduced, especially of snuff. One haul captured by the police looked like a cargo of oil cakes for cattle but turned out to be compressed cakes of snuff.

Even though patrols had been set up in the previous century by the Bow Street Runners the situation in London after the Napoleonic Wars was desperate. Citizens were not safe day or night on the streets of London. Robert Peel was appointed Secretary for Ireland, a post which he held from 1812 to 1818. Within that time he set up a regular Irish Constabulary the members of which were called Peelers after their founder. Peel was determined to introduce a similar system to London and he was also keen to revise the English criminal law, especially those parts dealing with capital offences. At that time there were over 200 offences, many of them trivial, for which the punishment was hanging.

The Honourable West India Company the trading company which used to control much of the export and import trade with the British West Indies **magistrate** an official who judges cases in the lowest courts of law, especially in police courts **Colquhoun** [kə'hu:n] **Wapping** ['wɒpɪŋ] area in east London; site of London's first police station, now a museum **Thames Division** the police department responsible for policing the River Thames **snuff** tobacco made into powder for sniffing into the nose **Bow Street Runners** (1749–1829) officers at Bow Street magistrates' court, London, whose duty was to chase and arrest criminals **the Napoleonic Wars** (1799–1815) the series of wars fought between France under Napoleon Bonaparte, and England, Prussia, Russia, and Austria **Secretary** *here:* minister in the British government **capital offence** crime for which people are executed

At last, when Peel became Home Secretary, the Metropolitan Police Bill was passed in 1829 and at the end of the year the Force officially came into being. The first 1,000 officers were grouped into six divisions and were controlled from a central office situated at No. 4 Whitehall Place which backed on to a courtyard known as Scotland Yard because Scottish kings used to stay there centuries ago. Although the official address of the newly formed police force was in Whitehall Place, behind the new headquarters, in Scotland Yard, was another building to which the public were usually referred. This was the Commissioner's Headquarters and most people and the Press began to refer to the police headquarters as Scotland Yard. In time the unofficial name became the official one and even today the main entrance to the present building is known as 'the Back Hall'.

Many of the original officers appointed were dismissed within a year for being drunk or corrupt. To lead the force Peel appointed two Commissioners, then termed justices, in the shape of Sir Charles Rowan who had served under the Duke of Wellington and Richard Mayne, son of an Irish judge, and a barrister in his own right. Together Rowan and Mayne evolved the principles on which they wished the new Force to base its work. Over a century and a half later these guidelines, known as the 'Primary Object', are still respected by every Metropolitan Police Officer:

> The primary object of an efficient Police is the prevention of crime; the next that of detection and punishment of offenders if crime is committed. To these ends all efforts of Police must be directed. The protection of life and property, the preservation of public tranquility, and the absence of crime will alone prove whether those efforts have been successful, and whether the objects for which the Police were appointed have been attained.

In spite of these ideals the new Police Force experienced much prejudice and dislike especially amongst the East Enders. The costers regarded them as enemies and did what they could to bring disgrace on the new regime. The uniform of the Police was at first top hat and tails and this alone made them look ridiculous. Soon a helmet replaced the hat, for practical as well as protective reasons, and a tunic replaced the coat tails. Truncheons were issued and to this day, except in special circumstances, this constitutes the

Home Secretary minister responsible for law and order, immigration control and other domestic matters **Metropolitan Police Bill** a proposed law to establish a police force for London **Commissioner** [kə'mɪʃnə] head of the Metropolitan Police **barrister** a lawyer who has the right to speak and argue in the higher courts of law **tranquility** peace, order **coster** ['kɒstə] (or costermonger); s. o. who sells fruit and vegetables from a stand in the street **top hat** a man's tall hat, often made of silk **tails** or tailcoat; a man's formal coat with a long shaped back, divided into 2 below the waist (See illustration p. 19) **tunic** a short coat worn as part of a uniform by policemen and soldiers **truncheon** a short thick stick carried as a weapon by policemen

NEW POLICE
A-LA-MILITAIRE!!

The police man – detested figure of authority

Felix Barker and Peter Jackson (1983), London: *2000 Years of a City and its People.* *(Cassell Ltd.*, London)

arms of an ordinary 'copper'. At an early stage too, they were issued with watches and whistles, much to the amusement of the populace. Soon musical hall artistes were singing songs about the Police and poking fun at the new regime. Songs that have entered the traditional stream are 'If you want to know the time ask a policeman', 'P. C. 49' and many others.

During Queen Victoria's reign the public attitude to the Police began to improve. When legislation was introduced to relieve the suffering of the

music(al) hall a type of theatre show with songs, humour and special acts **Queen Victoria** (1819–1901), Queen of Great Britain 1837–1901 **reign** [reɪn] a period in which s. o. is king or queen poor it fell on the Police to see that these social reforms were carried out. Thus they were in close contact with the poor, sick and needy and under orders to help where necessary. This in time endeared them to the people and it was realized that catching criminals was not their only concern. The Police in fact became the principal social and emergency services to the community.

Jean Harrowven (1983), *Origin and Tales of London Town.* Tadworth: Kaye and Ward. pp. 219–221.

Comprehension

Write a brief summary of the text. The answers to the following 'signpost questions' will provide you with a basic outline for your summary.

- Why and when were river patrols set up?
- What were Robert Peel's two main plans?
- Why was it necessary to introduce these plans?
- How were these plans realised?
- On what principles was the Metropolitan Police run?
- How did the relationship between the Metropolitan Police and the people of London develop?

Language skills

Devise a suitable title for each paragraph. Discuss your titles with the rest of the class and try to reach agreement as a class on one title for each paragraph.

Topic work

1. Imagine you are Robert Peel and that you have to write a newspaper article with the aim of convincing the public that a police force is necessary in London.
2. Discuss what are the most serious crimes in the place where you live and the ways the police try to deal with them. How effective is police action and what suggestions for improvement can you make?
3. What attitude do you and your fellow students have towards the police? How similar or different are these attitudes to those expressed in the text?

5. Victorian London

5.1 The Poor

In 1883 the chairman of the London School Board reported that out of three schools in the parish of Whitechapel that were surveyed with children from 1129 families, 871 families had only one room to live in and in the majority of cases the number of people sharing with them was as many as five and, in some cases, as high as nine. The broken windows were frequently stuffed with rags or covered with papers (they were rarely opened because of the smells outside, and because the wretches who lived in them were badly clothed and couldn't be exposed to draughts. In Wentworth Street, a daily procession of waggons carted their uncovered piles of rubbish to the dust destructor which Mrs Barnett renamed the dust distributor because of the clouds of dust it vomited out and the way it choked the drains). In some cases, these 'repairs' might be enough to justify the landlord's charging an extra threepence a week for rent! The average number of people in each room was generally between five and seven. In the house at 35 Hanbury Street, typical of the parish, there were seven people in each room with adult sons and daughters sleeping on the floor. In none of the rooms was there more than one bedstead, and the only w. c. was on the ground floor. This was normally in such a filthy state that the tenants used their chamber pots which, said the Rev R. C. Billing, giving evidence to a House of Commons Select Committee, were left in the rooms for a very long time before being taken down and emptied in the yard. Staircase banisters had often been removed for firewood and it was a common sight to see vermin-infested wallpaper hanging in strips from the walls. What furniture there was might consist of the broken-down remains of an old bed-

London School Board committee responsible for schools in London **to vomit** *here:* pour out suddenly with great force and in great quantity **landlord** a person from whom s.o. rents all or part of a building **threepence** ['θrepəns] **parish** a small area with its own government **chamber pot** a pot used at night instead of the w.c. **Rev** Reverend; title given to a priest **to give evidence** make a statement about a matter **House of Commons Select Committee** a small committee of about 12 members of the House of Commons which investigates a particular matter **vermin** unpleasant small insect or animal stead or table but was more likely a wooden board across some bricks, or an old hamper or box turned upside down; the bed might be a sack of flea-infested straw.

Andrew Mearns in *The Bitter Cry of Outcast London* pulled few punches:

> Every room in these rotten and reeking tenements houses a family, often two. In one cellar a sanitary inspector reports finding a father, mother, three children, and four pigs! In another room a missionary found a man ill with small-pox, his wife just recovering from her eighth confinement, and the children running about half naked and covered with dirt. Here are seven people living in one underground kitchen, and a little dead child lying in the same room. Elsewhere is a poor widow, her three children, and a child who had been dead thirteen days. Her husband, who was a cabman, had shortly before committed suicide. Here lives a widow and her six children, two of them who are ill with scarlet fever. In another, nine brothers and sisters, from 29 years of age downwards, live, eat and sleep together. Here is a mother who turns her children into the street in the early evening because she lets her room for immoral purposes until long after midnight, when the poor little wretches creep back again if they have not found some miserable shelter elsewhere. Where there are beds they are simply heaps of dirty rags, shavings or straw, but for the most part these miserable beings find rest only upon the filthy boards. The tenant of this room is a widow, who herself occupies the only bed, and lets the floor to a married couple for 2s. 6d. per week. In many cases matters are made worse by the unhealthy occupations followed by those who dwell in these habitations. Here you are choked as you enter by the air laden with particles of the superfluous fur pulled from the skins of rabbits, rats, dogs and other animals in their preparation for the furrier. Here the smell of paste and of drying match-boxes, mingling with other sickly odours, overpowers you; or it may be the fragrance of stale fish or vegetables, not sold on the previous day, and kept in the room overnight. Even when it is possible to do so the people seldom open their windows, but if they did it is questionable whether much would be gained, for the external air is scarcely less heavily charged with poison than the atmosphere within. ...

The commonest work was sweat-shop tailoring. For trouser finishing (sewing in linings, making button holes and stitching on the buttons) a

to infest cause trouble by being present in large numbers **hamper** a large basket with a lid used for carrying food **to pull punches** criticise less severely than deserved **tenement** a large building divided into flats **sanitary inspector** an official who is concerned with public health **small-pox** a serious infectious disease, causing spots which leave marks on the skin **confinement** the time during which a woman about to give birth is kept in bed **cabman** *here:* driver of a horse-drawn carriage for hire **to commit suicide** kill oneself **scarlet fever** a serious and easily-spread disease, marked by a painful throat and red spots **filthy** very dirty **habitation** a place where people live **to be choked** *here:* be prevented from breathing **laden with** loaded with **superfluous** not needed **furrier** ['fʌrɪə] a person who makes clothes using fur **sickly** causing a sick feeling **fragrance** smell **stale** no longer fresh **vegetable** ['vedʒtəbl] **charged with** loaded with **sweat-shop** [swet] factory or workshop where workers work long hours for low pay in bad conditions **sew** [səʊ] **lining** a piece of material covering the inside of a jacket, trousers, etc. **to stitch** sew woman might get twopence ha'penny a pair and have to buy her own thread. For making men's shorts they were paid tenpence a dozen, lawn tennis aprons threepence a dozen, and babies' hoods from 1s. 6d. to 2s. 6d. a dozen. In St George's-in-the-East women and children, some only seven years old, were employed as sackmakers and earning a farthing for each one they made. Sometimes women could earn a penny or twopence a peck by shelling peas, or twopence farthing a gross matchbox making, but out of this they would have to buy the string and the paste. None of these earnings would give them more than tenpence or a shilling a day, and might mean seventeen hours work.

Life in such circumstances had to be lived on a day-to-day or, better still, an hourly basis. Food was bought for immediate consumption. In one family, Booth found, they would buy nothing until it was actually needed. 'They go to their shop as an ordinary housewife to her canisters; twice a day they buy tea, or three times if they make it so often; in 35 days they made 72 purchases of tea, amounting in all to 5s. 2$\frac{3}{4}$d., and all most carefully noted down. The 'pinch of tea' costs $\frac{3}{4}$d. (no doubt this was $\frac{1}{2}$oz. at 2s. per lb.). Of sugar there were 77 purchases in the same time.'

Couples could struggle along on a hand to mouth existence until children came along. Most children were physically and mentally underdeveloped – that is, those who did not die in childbirth. Fifty-five per cent of East End children died before they were five. One-tenth of elementary school children were estimated later to be mentally defective or unnaturally dull. Children frequently came to school crying with hunger and fell off their seats from exhaustion. In winter they could not learn because they were too cold.

Donald Rumbelow (1988), *The Complete Jack the Ripper*. London: © W. H. Allen & Co.

twopence ['tʌpəns] **ha'penny** ['heɪpni] coin no longer in use (half a penny) **hood** a covering for the whole of the head and neck **farthing** a coin worth one quarter of a penny; no longer in use **on a day-to-day basis** planning for only one day at a time with little thought for the future **Booth** [bu:ð] Charles, author of two books on the condition of the poor in the East End of London **elementary school** old name for primary school

Comprehension

1. Why couldn't people living in the rooms described open their windows?
2. Why does the writer put the word 'repair' in inverted commas?
3. What did these 'repairs' consist of?
4. What did people in these rooms do if they wanted to go to the toilet?
5. Name five pieces of furniture that might be found in these rooms.
6. Name five ways in which the people in the rooms described by Andrew Mearns tried to earn money.
7. Name the garments which earned their makers the most and the least amount of money.
8. Why did people buy food in such small quantities?
9. Name five effects of the poverty on the children of these families.

Language skills

1. Use the information given in the excerpt to write a short report on 'Living conditions of the poor in the East End around 1880'.
2. Find words and phrases in the excerpt connected with the topics 'dirt and pollution'.

Topic work

In the Victorian age the most popular theory used to explain poverty and the misery associated with it was that of 'urban degeneration'. According to this theory the causes of poverty were the pressures of city existence, since

> "crammed together in filthy airless, and noisy one-room tenements, it was inevitable that the poor should be brutalized and sexually immoral and that they should seek to escape the dreadful monotony of their existence by craving the 'cheap excitements' offered by the pubs, the low music halls and the streets ... The savage and brutalized condition of the casual poor was the result of long exposure to the degenerating conditions of city life." (Gareth Steadman-Jones, *Outcast London,* p. 286)

How far do you think that this theory is a convincing explanation of the conditions described in the excerpt? What other causes for these conditions can you put forward?

(*Cassell Ltd.*, London)

5.2 The Mob

... Throughout most of the nineteenth century, there was no widespread awareness amongst the propertied and the powerful of the fact that the growth of the metropolis, the speculative housing system, the destruction of slums to build new roads and allow in railways, the creation of the East End, the undermining of traditional industries and the rise of sweated and casual labour, had contributed to generate a kind of urban desolation on a scale never before known.

But in 1886, the complacency of the fashionable West End appeared for a few days to be directly threatened by what was referred to as 'the mob'. On Monday, 8 February, during a bitterly cold winter which had put many Londoners in the building trades and the docks out of work, a demonstration was organized in Trafalgar Square. A crowd of about twenty thousand, many of them reportedly dockers and building workers from

mob a large and violent crowd **widespread** *here:* found among many people **awareness** knowledge **speculative housing** houses built, often in large numbers, not to order but for sale on the open market **undermining** weakening **sweated** forced to work long hours for little money **casual** [kæʒʊəl] being employed for only a short time **urban** belonging to a town or city **desolation** G. Trostlosigkeit **on a scale** G. in einem Umfang **complacency** being satisfied with things as they are **reportedly** [rɪˈpɔːtɪdli] the suburbs, turned up. *The Times* reported that: 'Their numbers were increased by a very great many of the idle class – of that large body in London who are spoken of by workers themselves as the class who want no work to do.'

The demonstrators demanded employment and were addressed with revolutionary rhetoric by Ben Tillett, the dockers' leader, and John Burns from the Social Democratic Federation, a militant socialist group. An attempt was made to wind up the demonstration in an orderly fashion, but a breakaway group headed for Pall Mall. Stones were thrown at the Carlton Club windows, and several were broken. Nobody is quite sure what happened. But one witness, the Socialist Henry Hyndman, later acquitted at the Old Bailey for his part in the riot, said that the Reform Club staff had thrown nailbrushes and shoes at the demonstrators. In retaliation, the windows of a number of clubs were broken with cobble stones picked up from St James's Street, which was being repaired.

The angry crowd continued to Hyde Park, smashing windows of fashionable shops, and turning over the carriages, in one case stripping the coachman of his livery and taking his place on the box. Big West End stores like Marshall & Snelgrove and Peter Robinson also suffered broken windows. The demonstrators marched home with their pickings from the West End singing 'Rule Britannia', but the fear of the mob did not lift for several days.

W. H. Smith, founder of the bookshop chain and then a Member of Parliament, told the Commons that it was 'almost incredible that, for at least an hour, the most frequented streets in the West End of London should be entirely at the mercy of the mob'. His sentiments were shared by many others. A dense fog descended on London and, frightened of a repetition of the disorder, shopkeepers and some householders shuttered their windows. Wild rumours spread of a vast army coming out of the East to

to turn up *here:* arrive **idle** ['aɪdəl] *here:* unemployed **to wind up** [waɪnd] *here:* bring to an end **a breakaway group** a smaller group which leaves a larger group **Pall Mall** [pælmæl] a street in London noted for its many clubs **Carlton Club** a club frequented by members of the Conservative Party **to acquit** [ə'kwɪt] say that s.o. is not guilty of a crime **Old Bailey** the main criminal court in England **Reform Club** a club frequented by members of the Liberal Party **retaliation** replying to one wrong by another **cobble stones** round stones used to cover the surface of a road **to strip** *here:* pull the clothes off s.o. **livery** special uniform for servants employed by the same person **pickings** *here:* things stolen **Rule Britannia** a very patriotic song, almost a second national anthem **incredible** too strange to be believed **to shutter** put a wooden or metal cover over a window **rumour** talk which is probably not true **vast** very large attack the West. Then the fog lifted, and with it the fear that London would be overturned by the downtrodden mass of its labouring classes. The crowd had never held any real threat of revolution, but the complacency of the West End had been shaken.

In fact, it now seems astonishing how those in power were willing to risk a mass revolt of the capital's working class rather than make concessions. For all the conditions were there for revolt: dreadful poverty, once highly skilled artisans reduced to 'sweated', lowly-paid labourers, and radical movements led by disenchanted workers whose interests were utterly opposed to those in power.

Gavin Weightman and Steve Humphries (1983), *The Making of Modern London 1815–1914*. London: Sidgwick and Jackson. pp. 150–3.

to overturn *here:* bring the present state to an end **downtrodden** treated badly by those in power **artisan** [a:tɪ'zæn] a skilled workman **disenchanted** feeling angry and bitter

Comprehension

What evidence is there in the text that the following statements are true? If there is no evidence explain what the passage really says.

1. The West End was the part of London inhabited by the rich, the powerful and the propertied.
2. The inhabitants of the West End were concerned that so many people had been made unemployed.
3. The leaders of the demonstration encouraged the demonstrators to riot and attack property in the West End.
4. It is possible that it was not the demonstrators who started the violence.
5. The mob sang 'Rule Britannia' to show people that they had nothing to fear from them.
6. People found it hard to believe that such violence could happen because they had never seen the living conditions in the East End.
7. After the demonstration on 8 February 1886 wealthy people were less satisfied with the state of society than they were before.
8. Those in power were more willing to make concessions to the poor after the riot on 8 February 1886.

Language skills

1. To understand a long complex sentence like the first one in the passage, it is sometimes useful to break it down into shorter sentences. This can be done by asking the question: "What were the propertied and powerful not aware of?"
   Give four answers to this question in your own words e.g.: They were not aware that the metropolis had grown.
2. The word 'but' is used to introduce a sentence or clause which contrasts with what has been said or written in the preceding sentence or clause. Often 'but' also points to the unexpected and surprising nature of this contrast. Find pairs of sentences linked by 'but' in this passage and explain the linkage.

Topic work

Imagine you are one of the workers who took part in the demonstration at Trafalgar Square on 8 February 1886. Write down what drove you to go there, what your feelings were as you listened to the speeches by Ben Tillett and Joe Burns and then saw the luxury of the West End around you. Finally, give your thoughts on the actions of the breakaway group.

6. Jack the Ripper

When George Cross walked through dark and empty Buck's Row on his way to work about 3.40 a.m. on the morning of Friday, 31 August 1888, the only light was a solitary gas lamp at the far end of the street. On one side of the street was a warehouse wall, and on the other some terrace houses which were occupied for the most part by better-class tradesmen. He was opposite these houses when, in a gateway leading to some stables, between the houses and the board school, he saw a bundle that he at first thought was a tarpaulin. It was only when he crossed over for a closer look that he realised the bundle was in fact a woman. She was lying on her back with one hand nearly touching the stable gate and the other her black straw bonnet, which was lying close by. Her skirt was pushed up almost to her waist. His first thought was that she had been raped and was still unconscious from the attack; and his next that he might have disturbed her attacker. Normally there was a great deal of noise in the street, but at that hour of the morning it was unusually quiet and although he listened carefully for any strange noises he could hear none. If he had disturbed the woman's attacker he must have heard his footsteps as he escaped or, supposing that the woman had been brought there in a cab and dumped, the rattle of wheels as he drove off. He was still by the body when he heard footsteps behind him.

John Paul, also a market porter, was likewise on his way to work when he saw Cross standing in the roadway. He stepped off the pavement to avoid him, but as he did so Cross touched him on the shoulder and said 'Come and look at this woman'. Paul cautiously did so but when Cross suggested that he should give him a hand to lift the woman to her feet, thinking she was only drunk, Paul refused to help him. Instead he knelt down and felt the woman's face and hands, which were already cold. He said that he thought she was dead but, as he straightened her clothes to make her a little more decent, he felt her heart and thought that he could detect a slight movement. Both men thought that the best thing they could do was to find a policeman, and they walked off together in search of one. Because it was so dark, neither had noticed the blood, now concealed by the skirt, coagulating on the pavement between the woman's legs.

Police Constable John Neil missed seeing them by minutes. Nearly half an hour had passed since he had last walked through Buck's Row, although his beat was a short one and could be covered at a brisk walk in twelve minutes. Shining his bull's-eye lamp into the stable gateway he saw what the two men had not been able to see, that the woman had been murdered. Blood was oozing from an ugly gash in her throat, which had been cut almost from ear to ear.

The windpipe and gullet had been completely severed, cut back to the spinal cord. Her eyes were open, and her skirt was rumpled above her knees; though her hands and wrists were cold, her arms – which he knelt down and felt – were still warm from the elbow upwards. The flashing of his lamp as he examined the body attracted the constable on an adjoining beat, and Neil called to him to run and fetch a doctor. There was a surgery close by and within quarter of an hour a Dr Llewellyn had been roused and was at the scene. He made a cursory examination of the body, watched by several policemen who obligingly shone their lamps on the body, and two or three men who having just finished work at a nearby slaughterhouse were on their way home.

Donald Rumbelow (1988), *The Complete Jack the Ripper*.

The first victim, Polly Nicholls

Felix Barker and Peter Jackson (1983), London: *2000 Years of a City and its People.* (*Cassell Ltd.*, London)

Comprehension

What evidence is there in the passage that the following statements are true? If you don't think a statement is true explain what really happened.

1. George Cross was a market porter.
2. George Cross was walking along the side of the street opposite the warehouse wall.
3. The body of the woman was on the other side of the street from George Cross.
4. George Cross thought he might have disturbed the woman's attacker because he heard footsteps.
5. John Paul wanted to avoid George Cross because he thought he might attack him.
6. John Paul thought that the woman was drunk.
7. If PC John Neil had covered his beat at normal speed he would have seen Cross and Paul.
8. Dr Llewellyn had been called by Cross and Paul.

Language skills

Write a report that PC Neil might have written at the police station after this incident. Include what he might have written down after having interviewed George Cross and John Paul.

Topic work

After reading the passages in 5.1 Victorian London – The Poor, p. 21 discuss what connection might exist between the conditions described in them and the murders committed by Jack the Ripper.

7. London at War

Saturday, 7 September 1940 is a day etched into the memory of many East End families. At around five o'clock on a hot, summery afternoon they were drawn onto the streets by the approaching roar of several hundred bombers. Most of them thought the planes were British for they had come to believe that the capital was no longer vulnerable to such an air attack.

Then the bombs began to fall, first on the Arsenal in Woolwich, then thousands raining down on the vast complex of docks on both sides of the Thames – especially the Victoria & Albert, the East India and the Surrey Commercial – setting them ablaze.

Very quickly people crouched in the official street shelters, or in their own living rooms, realized that they too were targets as the maze of narrow streets and blocks of flats from West Ham to Bow, from Bermondsey to Whitechapel and from Limehouse to Poplar were blitzed. One of those standing in King Street, Poplar was eighteen-year-old Len Jones:

That afternoon, around five o'clock, I went outside the house, I'd heard the aircraft, and it was very exciting, because the first formations were coming over without any bombs dropping, but very, very majestic; terrific. And I had no thought that they were actually bombers. Then from that point on I was well aware, because bombs began to fall, and shrapnel was going along King Street, dancing off the cobbles. Then the real impetus came, in so far as the suction and the compression from the high explosive blasts just pulled you and pushed you, and the whole of this atmosphere was turbulating so hard that, after an explosion of a nearby bomb, you could actually feel your eyeballs being sucked out. I was holding my eyes to try and stop them going. And the suction was so vast, it ripped my shirt away, and ripped my trousers. Then I couldn't get my breath, the smoke was like acid and everything round me was black and yellow. And these bombers just kept on and on, the whole road was moving, rising and falling.

The first wave of bombs was hitting the poorest and most overcrowded parts of London and some slum buildings, like the jerry-built tenements of Canning Town, disintegrated into rubble, burying their occupants underneath. In the shelters, there were men and women shouting and screaming hysterically as each blast rocked the very structures that were protecting them. London was experiencing its first mass air attack by the Luftwaffe.

The East End faced the full brunt of this attack. The first instinct of Gladys Strelitz and her family in East Ham was to run away from the bombs:

We had been bombed all day long and there was a lull. My brother said, 'Come on girls, get all the children's clothes in a bag and we've got to get out of London, there is a lull.' And so we got this bus, and we went to Bow. And when we got to Bow the bombing was going so badly that the conductor pulled the bell and said that we wouldn't go any further. So the only place to go was to run under this crypt, under this big church. And there the sight that met my eyes, it overcome me. Because there was people praying, and crying and asking God to help us, because there was bombs going on and this crypt, it was actually shuddering. And, well, it was too much for me, I just passed out.

Len Jones ran into a nearby street shelter in Poplar, which he was to share with several Chinese families that lived in the area:

The shelter was brick and concrete built, and it was lifting and moving, rolling almost as if it was a ship in a rough sea. And the suction and the blasts coming in and out of this

cobbles round stones used to cover the surface of a road **turbulating** moving violently and irregularly **jerry-built** built using cheap materials **the full brunt** G. 'die volle Wucht' **lull** intervall of quiet **overcome** dialect and nonstandard past tense for overcame **there was + plural** colloquial and nonstandard usage **shuddering** shaking violently **Poplar** part of the East End of London, near the old docks

> steel door, which was smashing backwards and forwards, bashed us around against the walls. The extent of injuries at that stage was just abrasions really, the shoulders and chest getting crushed against the wall, or across the floor. The worst part was the poor little kids; they were so scared, they were screaming and crying, clutching at their parents. The heat was colossal, the steel door was so hot you couldn't touch it. And everybody was being sick and people were carrying out their normal human needs, and the smell was terrible.

The second attack came later that evening and continued into the early hours of Sunday morning. By this time 430 East Enders had died – many corpses lay in the streets and gardens. Sixteen hundred were seriously injured, and tens of thousands were made homeless. Len Jones was shocked by what he saw when he emerged from his street shelter early that morning:

> I went out to see how our house was, and when I got there the front door was lying back, and the glass of the windows had fallen in, and I could see the top of the house had virtually disappeared. Inside, everything was blown to pieces, you could see it all by the red glow reflecting from the fires that were raging outside. Then I looked out the back and suddenly I realized that where my father's shed and workshop used to be, was just a pile of rubble, bricks. Then I saw two bodies, two heads sticking up, I recognized one head in particular; it was a Chinese man, Mr Say, he had one eye closed, and then I began to realize that he was dead.

Joanna Mack and Steve Humphries (1985), *The Making of Modern London 1939–1945: London at War.* London: London Weekend Television.

abrasion [ə'breɪʒən] place where the skin has been scratched away **virtually** ['vɜ:tʃʊəli] almost completely

Language skills

Make a list of all the descriptions of the seven events in the excerpt listed below, putting them into five categories according to the way they have been perceived: seen; heard; touched; smelt; sense of direction or movement.
Discuss your list with those of your fellow students and try to reach agreement on your categories.

1. The bombers approach (para. 1)
2. The bombs begin to fall (paras. 2 + 3)
3. Len Jones' personal narrative (para. 3)
4. The effects of the bombing (para. 4)
5. Gladys Strelitz's description of the crypt (para. 5)
6. The scene in the shelter in Poplar (para. 6)
7. The second attack (para. 7)

Topic work

Describe a real or imaginary event similar to that of the bombing raid in the text. Two possibilities are a car accident or a house fire. Write your description in the first person and try to enable the reader to see, feel, hear, taste and smell what you did, what happened to you or what you imagined.

LIVING AND WORKING IN LONDON

London, that great sea, whose ebb and flow
At once is deaf and loud, and on the shore
Vomits its wrecks, and still howls on for more,
Yet in its depths what treasures!

Percy Bysshe Shelley (1792–1822)

1. London's Lonesome Cowboys

There are 20,000 motorbike messengers in London speeding through the streets like demented aliens. Who are the people who choose to spend their lives like this? Peter Crookston reports

It's raining all over London. Wet from Woolwich to Wimbledon, Bermondsey to Balham. Gary, the taxi driver's son, eases his motor bike into the gap between a bus and a lorry in SE23 and waits, dripping, for the lights to change. Hazel, Bachelor of Science (Imperial College), remembers the treachery of the surface on the Blackwall Tunnel approach and throttles back her Honda CX500. Gabriel, former teacher of European history, hunches behind the meagre shelter of his windshield as he sluices along the M4 to the airport. Michael, middle-aged ex-public schoolboy, remembers sodden expeditions at

demented mad, crazy **alien** *here:* s.th. totally different from what is normal **to ease** move carefully **Bachelor of Science** (B.Sc.) first degree in science at British universities **Imperial College** a college forming part of the University of London **treachery** *here:* dangerous nature **Blackwall Tunnel** a tunnel under the River Thames **to hunch** pull your back into a rounded shape **meagre** G. spärlich **to sluice along** [slu:s] *here:* drive fast through the wet **the M4** a motorway leading out of London to the west **ex-** former **public schoolboy** a boy who went to a public (i.e. not part of the state system) school

Gordonstoun and groans behind the misted visor of his crash helmet as he leans into the Hanger Lane gyratory system.

But a day like this is a small price to pay for freedom ... the freedom to ride a bike and be paid for it, to work as hard as you like, to take holidays whenever you feel like it, to pile up money for a winter in Spain. So you'd better work today, in the January rain and wind, because it's on days like this that you're in demand – the days when the office cars get stuck in traffic, when the secretaries won't walk from one end of Regent Street to the other, when the Gidea Park to Liverpool Street is cancelled.

These are the days, in fact, when everyone needs ... a despatch rider.

'We'll send a bike ...' 'It's coming DR ...' 'A rider's on his way ...' 'It's on wheels now ...'

How easy it is to simply pick up the phone and call Delta, Pony Express, Chameleon, Fleet Street Flyers, Prontobike, West One, CSL, On Yer Bike, Inter City, Arrowfast or Apollo. To quote your company's computer-coded number to Jenny, Tracy, Sharon or Liz and hear their efficient, ever-so-helpful voices tell you that a bike will be with you soonest: five, maybe ten, certainly not longer than 20 minutes.

Now you can relax, for here he is, scarcely audible behind his knightly helmet, marvellously ill-favoured from the pelting weather, your winged Mercury from beyond the double glazing. Words are hardly necessary, for he knows your commands. The little black radio receiver on his shoulder has told him all he needs to know; Jenny, Tracy, Sharon or Liz have faithfully relayed your instructions. Just smile, say something sympathetic about the rain, and put your package in his outstretched gauntlet.

He may impress you by flinging himself through the swing doors and running down the stairs, showering passers-by with scattered drops. Extreme, you may think, for an errand to the depths of the Middle Temple. But what you don't know is that your hurrying messenger is paid by the number of jobs he packs into the day, that he might be earning a lot more than you, and maybe even more than your boss.

Gordonstoun ['gɔ:dənstən] a public school in Scotland, attended by Prince Charles **Hanger Lane** a main road in west London **gyratory system** G. Kreisverkehr **to be in demand** wanted by a lot of people **to cancel** G. ausfallen lassen **despatch rider** s.o. who carries messages on a motor cycle **ill-favoured** *here:* looking unattractive **pelting** *here:* with rain falling heavily **Mercury** the Roman name for Hermes, the messenger god, with winged sandals **double glazing** windows with two sheets of glass **gauntlet** a long glove covering the wrist **errand** a short journey to get s.th. or carry a message **the Middle Temple** one of the four legal societies in London which form the Inns of Court: a law school

'We reckon that a busy, experienced rider with a good knowledge of London can make £250 to £300 a week,' says John Hutchinson, the 40-year-old, fast-talking, transport manager of Delta, the company with the largest fleet of despatch riders in the metropolitan area.

Mr Hutchinson, who started as a minicab driver, keeps up a running commentary of facts and figures as he shows off Delta's new office block at Park Royal, in northwest London. 'We have 120 riders here, all self-employed, paying their own income tax and National Insurance. They have to supply their own machines, and many of them have two so that they're not off the road if one breaks down. We insist that their machines are at least 250 cc and not more than three years old. They have to tax and insure their bikes, but we have the renewal dates on computer so that we can remind them and keep everything legal. We supply the riders with bibs in our own livery, and provide panniers and a top box, for their bikes.

'Our biggest accounts are with London Weekend Television, Channel 4, DHL, the airfreight company, and TV-am. They give us so much work that they each have a special hot line to us, whereby they simply pick up a telephone to get us on the other end.

Peter Slemming, managing director of West One, thinks that most despatch riders have a love affair with their bikes. 'They practically live on them. When they're not working for us they take their holidays riding around the Continent. And when the bike races are on in France, I just know I'm going to be short of about 25 riders that week.'

One of his most dedicated and efficient riders is a man with one arm. Will Watson, 27, from Bury St Edmunds, Suffolk, lost his right arm before he became a despatch rider, when he was learning to ride a motor bike and had a crash with a car nine years ago. It took him three years to get back on the road, with a disabled rider's licence and on a bike with specially adapted controls so that he can operate clutch,

minicab a small car used as a taxi **National Insurance** money paid to the government which is used for pensions, sick pay and unemployment benefit **renewal date** date when the money for tax and insurance has to be paid again **bib** *here:* cloth tied to the body with the name of the company written on it **livery** ['lɪvərɪ] *here:* special badge or sign of a company **pannier** ['pænɪə] bag or box carried on the side of a bicycle or motor cycle **account** *here:* business dealings **London Weekend Television** the commercial television company which transmits programmes in the London area at weekends **hot line** a direct telephone connection **managing director** s.o. who manages a company **dedicated** giving all his energy and interest to his work **clutch** G. Kupplung throttle and front brake with his left hand. He locks his artificial hand to the right side of the handlebars with its spring-loaded thumb.

Will is an archetypal old-style biker: long black hair gathered pirate-fashion into a bunch at the back, bushy black beard, studs in one ear and a ring though his nose. It takes him an hour and 50 minutes to ride up to London before he begins thrashing around the West End and City on his errands. In January he struggled in through the snow.

He was the only biker who did not disparage despatch riding as a career. Perhaps for him, given his disability and his obsession about biking, it is the ideal career. And luckily he's in a growth industry. All the bike operators in London say they can't get enough riders to cope with the volume of work. People who only a few years ago thought a despatch rider was someone in the army, now find they can't live without them. Hello, Jenny, Sharon, Tracy, Liz ... send us Gary, Gabby, Hazel, Mike or Will.

Fear not, dear caller ... they will not let you down. Just think of trusty Will, riding stiff-backed and straggle-bearded through the swirling snow from Suffolk, his plastic arm locked to the handlebars, his eyes fixed Londonwards, where he comes to do your bidding.

Jenny, one of Chameleon's team of 14 riders. The money's good but is it a career?

The Mail on Sunday, 'You' Magazine, date not known.

throttle G. Gashebel **handlebar** G. Lenker **archetypal** ['a:kɪtaɪpəl] a perfect example of s.th. **stud** *here:* small piece of metal **to thrash** *here:* drive very fast **to disparage** [dɪs'pærɪdʒ] make s.th. sound unimportant, of little value **obsession** a fixed idea which you can't stop thinking about **to cope with** deal successfully with **straggle-bearded** with a long, untidy beard **swirling** blowing in all directions **Suffolk** ['sʌfək] a county to the north-east of London

Comprehension

1. What disadvantages connected with the job of despatch rider are mentioned in the article?
2. What are the motives of the people who become despatch riders?
3. Why is there a great demand for despatch riders when the weather is bad?
4. Why don't the customers of the despatch riders need to talk to them very much?
5. What conditions are imposed on the despatch riders?
6. What does Delta do for its riders?
7. Explain what is meant by a 'hot line'.
8. What does Peter Slemming mean when he says that most despatch riders 'have a love affair with their bikes'?
9. How does the writer show that Will Watson is a specially enthusiastic despatch rider?

Topic work

1. Pair work; one student takes the part of a journalist and interviews another student who takes the part of a despatch rider, Keep a record of your questions and the answers you receive and compare them with those of the other students.
2. What is your opinion of the life of a despatch rider? Say why this kind of job would or would not appeal to you.

2. Little Beggars

Slouched in sleeping bags, dreaming of making it in the capital, more and more children and teenagers are begging on the streets of London.

Following the April social security cuts, it seems there is now no legal income for the majority of 16- and 17-year-olds who are not in work or on YTS schemes.

And this, says Nick Hardwick, director of Centrepoint, the West End emergency youth shelter, is most of the explanation for the dozens of cupped-hand youths now haunting the Tube; the other factor being the increasing rarity of cheap accommodation. "The stereotype might be that they are lazy and idle, but these kids are often more enterprising and less apathetic than those who stay behind. The majority have come to the capital seeking work. They've taken Norman Tebbit's advice and got on their bikes." Their begging, he says, will generally be short-term, aimed at acquiring the cash to afford somewhere to live. Without an address, many employers will not entertain a young applicant. Others get hooked and dragged down by their begging. What was a temporary expedient becomes a habit.

If the intention has been to cure these young people of any incipient benefit dependency, it seems to have worked. Many can no longer be bothered to claim now. "But instead of the benefits culture," notes Hardwick, "what is developing is a pretty degrading street culture that is actually much more damaging."

Drug-dealing, burglary, robbery and prostitution are the more extreme stratagems for survival. Hanging around the back of supermarkets at garbage time will usually

slouched sitting with round shoulders and looking tired **to make it** be successful **YTS** Youth Training Scheme **emergency** in a dangerous or hopeless situation **enterprising** able to think of s.th. to do **apathetic** [æpə'θetɪk] without interest, not able to do anything **Norman Tebbit** former Conservative Secretary for Employment; he said that when his father was unemployed in the 1930s he "got on his bike" to look for a job **to entertain** *here:* think about employing **expedient** [ɪk'spi:diənt] plan **incipient** [ɪn'sɪpiənt] at an early stage **benefit** money received from the government **dependency** being influenced or controlled by s.th. or s.o. **to be bothered to do s.th.** make the effort to do s.th. **benefits culture** a way of life dependent on social security benefits **degrading** bringing down to a lower level **burglary** stealing s.th. from a house **stratagem** a trick, plan **survival** continuing to live **to hang around** wait

Zach Doyle, aged 19, on the London Underground (Brian Moody)

provide something useful. Or those with a special thirst might act the part of waiter in a station bar and make off with trays of half-supped drinks. The one option most of the West End young take up, if only part-time, is begging. It is probably the most educational, both for what it tells them about their own condition and what it teaches them about the public.

A couple of youths at Tottenham Court Road – one from Torbay, the other from Dublin – said it was "the coloureds" who gave most, "maybe because they've gone through a lot and so they understand more than other people do." White working-class young men showed the ugliest disposition, they said. Both the youths were on "the tap" full-time, and said they could count on £20 to £30 a day, depending on how often the police moved them on. Irish Zach had had a bad day: £7, even though it had been an early start and he had covered most of the central station areas.

For Mancunian Darren, "middle-class people are the best, the ones who've just got a cosy house with a few kids. But all these yuppies, you know what I mean, with briefcases, they look at you like you're a piece of dog dirt."

He admits, though, he does not have "the guts" to beg successfully. Every instant is a torment and even when he crawls for comfort inside the same bag as his mate Steph, he still hides his face and will not say a word.

to take up choose **Torbay** a town in south-west England **on the tap** (slang) begging **Mancunian** [mæn'kju:nɪən] s.o. from Manchester **cosy** ['kəʊzi] pleasant, comfortable **kid** (slang) child **yuppies** ['jʌpi] young urban professionals: young people with good jobs and a lot of money **briefcase** a flat case for carrying papers **guts** (slang) courage **Steph** [sti:v] Stephen

Fourteen-year-old Darren has lived on London's streets for 18 months
(Brian Moody)

Steph, just 15, seems to have a scheme for everything. Darren walks about town on his blistered feet and his one set of filthy clothes. Steph has a young woman friend at the back of Covent Garden who will wash his clothes and have him over for a night of video-viewing. Darren counts himself lucky if he makes £10 for a full day's begging. Steph can top £100; £300 on a Saturday. I witnessed him hauling the handfuls of pound coins – £130 in seven hours – from his pockets, and his attempts to change them into notes at local theatres and arcades before sweet-talking a girl at a Leicester Square *bureau de change*: he tipped her £1.50.

The secret of Steph's success is that he understands market forces. His extreme youth and open, wounded face, the pathetically scrawled sign that pleads for relief: all make him a product the travelling consumer cannot resist. And he understands how to operate the levers of guilt. Since youth is the essence, his powers to move them will decline with each passing month. For now, though, "I just have to look at them, yeah, and one out of every three collapses with guilt. You hear them talking as they walk by. But I can't do that, look at them. Because I know what I do is dead disgusting, dead bad. And I hate it. But I admit it does get easier and sometimes after a while I can put my head up and just laugh.

blistered with painful swellings **filthy** very dirty **Covent Garden** district in Central London **to count o.s. lucky** consider, think o.s. lucky **to top** get more than **to haul** pull **arcade** *here:* G. Spielhalle **to sweet-talk** talk nicely to s.o. in order to get s.th. **bureau de change** place where you can change foreign currency **wounded** hurt **to scrawl** write **to plead** G. flehen **relief** help **consumer** s.o. who buys and uses goods and services **lever** ['li:və] long piece of metal used to move or operate s.th. **essence** most important thing **yeah** (coll.) yes **to collapse** *here:* become helpless

Sometimes I've got to talk to them too because I can't sit all day ... It physically hurts just sitting there."

Like Darren he is the product of a dislocated home life. Dad, a prosperous timber merchant in their small town near Inverness, left the family when Steph was 12. He sees his dad as a man who "talks through money", always handing him fistfuls of coins that he kept in sweet jars. Even when the police returned Steph to him earlier this year, he says his dad uttered scarcely a line – "Howya doing?" – before reaching into his wallet. His mother, though, weeps for him to come home. He phones her occasionally and she will come hunting him in London. But he says it is all too late. What he wants now is his own place and a chance for stability.

Andrew Tyler, *The Independent Magazine* 3 December 1988.

dead (coll.) completely, absolutely **dislocated** G. durcheinandergebracht **prosperous** having a lot of money **timber** wood **Inverness** town in Scotland **howya** (coll.) how are you **wallet** [wɒlɪt] G. Brieftasche

Comprehension

1. What are the two reasons why young people are begging in the Underground?
2. Why should Nick Hardwick think that the young people begging are more enterprising and less apathetic than other young people without work?
3. Why should it be damaging to young people to reduce state benefits?
4. What do Darren and Steph learn about their own condition and the public through begging?
5. Why is Steph successful and Darren unsuccessful at begging?

Language skills

The writer uses many colloquial, figurative, and slang expressions in this article. Rewrite the phrases in italics in your own words.

1. 'They've taken Norman Tebbit's advice and *got on their bikes*.' (l. 24/25)
2. 'The secret of Steph's success is that *he understands market forces*.' (l. 110/111)
3. 'All make him a *product the travelling consumer cannot resist*.' (l. 115/116)
4. 'And he understands how to *operate the levers of guilt*.' (l. 116–118)
5. ' one out of three *collapses with guilt*.' (l. 122–124)
6. 'He sees his dad as a man who *'talks through money'*.' (l. 138–140)

Topic work

1. Compare the characters of Steph and Darren and their attitude to begging and life in London.
2. Work in groups of two or three for this task. One or two students should take the part of reporters who interview the other, playing the part of Steph. Discuss the results of the interviews in class.
3. Using words and expressions from the article write a short report on the situation of young unemployed people in your own country.

3. The Tower Block: Dream or Nightmare?

But very quickly the high-rise dream went wrong. It soon became clear that many Londoners hated living in the new tower blocks. Politicians and planners who commissioned them had been seduced by a numbers game which gave impressive rehousing figures but created untold human misery. However, this rejection of high rise was not as simple and uniform as we now often imagine. The luxurious and spacious interiors of the flats were welcomed, especially by those who had just escaped from tenement slums. Some towers, which were well designed and enjoyed strong tenants' associations and good caretakers, were very popular amongst residents. But there were two serious grievances that quickly turned many tenants against the tower blocks. The first concerned the lifts, which were too few, too small and too slow. Worst of all they were constantly breaking down and could easily be vandalised. And because of a shortage of money for back-up, the tiny management and maintenance staff of the GLC often took a long time to put things right. This hadn't been a problem in the flats built in the 1950s, which were generally much lower and often had stairs as opposed to lifts. Lift break-downs meant that those living on the upper levels faced exhausting journeys up and down hundreds of stairs to get in and out. For the old, the sick and mothers with young children, these long climbs were an appalling prospect. The break-downs resulted in some people being stranded for hours or occasionally days. Doreen Reid lived on one of the top floors of a high-rise block in Plaistow with her husband and baby Tracy in the late 1960s:

> The first problem I discovered was the lifts; that was the first nasty experience. I had a rather large pram for Tracy when she was a baby. I went out one day and I came back and my lift wasn't working. Well, I had twenty-four flights of stairs to get up to my flat. It was very, very hard work and took me ages. I had visions of Tracy coming out of

nightmare a bad dream **high-rise** built very high **tower block** a tall block of flats or offices **to be seduced by s.th.** *here:* persuaded by s.th. which seems attractive **rehousing figures** numbers of people put into new houses **untold** so great that it cannot be expressed **luxurious** very comfortable **spacious** ['speɪʃəs] with a lot of room **tenement** large building divided into flats lived in by poor people **association** a society or club, formed for a special purpose **caretaker** a person who looks after a school or other large building **to vandalise** damage or destroy **back-up** support **as opposed to** in contrast to **Plaistow** [plæstəʊ or pla:stəʊ (the local pronunciation)] a district in east London **I had visions of** I could imagine

'Wave Bye Bye to Gran'
Clifford Lines and Laurie Bolwell (1987), *Geography GCSE.* London: Letts. p. 49. (*Punch Publications Ltd.*)

> the pram, my shopping going everywhere and I didn't attempt it again after that. So if the lift wasn't working then I just couldn't go out at all. I was virtually in the flat all the time until the lift was going. Sometimes it would take a day, sometimes two days, and I just couldn't get out at all because to take baby out in the pram was impossible.

The second grievance came specifically from families with young children, who found the tower blocks totally unsuited to their needs. Lack of play space for children inside and outside the towers created a claustrophobic atmosphere. It was impossible to supervise children's outdoor play and mothers were terrified at the prospect of their children falling off balconies, out of windows, or down stairs. Doreen Reid:

> There was virtually nowhere for Tracy, or any other child, to play. Our block was on a main road, so you had the traffic down there. The only place she could play basically was in her bedroom or the lounge area. The only time I could open the balcony door was if I was in the room with her continually because with young children, when they're growing up, they're into everything. I couldn't let her out – but I got neighbours complaining if she made too much noise indoors, like the tenant underneath or

virtually almost **claustrophobic** [klɔ:strəˈfəʊbɪk] making you feel frightened because you are in a small, closed space **supervise** [ˈsu:pəvaɪz] **lounge** [laʊndʒ] a comfortable room for sitting in

In 1968 Ronan Point tower block in Newham collapsed, killing five people. This tragedy brought the brief heyday of the tower block to an end (*Keystone Pressedienst,* Hamburg)

the tenant upstairs. I remember one day I was out in the kitchen doing some hand-washing, and I thought to myself 'Tracy's quiet, what's she up to?' And I called out to her and I got no answer. I thought, 'That's not like her.' I wandered into the lounge and it was then I realized that the balcony door was open, and I thought 'Oh no!' I just went cold, literally cold; I stepped out onto the balcony, and I instinctively looked over the top because I fully expected to find Tracy at the bottom. When I looked down and found she wasn't there I came in and I looked in my bedroom first; she wasn't there, and then I went into her bedroom and there she was playing with her toys. But at the time it gave me a very very bad fright.

But what really brought the brief heyday of the tower block to an end was its terrible structural defects. Some of the towers were inadequately tested and built to unsafe heights. In 1968 disaster struck when Ronan Point, a brand new block of system-built flats in Newham, partially collapsed, killing five people.

Steve Humphries and John Taylor (1986), *The Making of Modern London 1945–1985*. London: London Weekend Television.

to be up to s.th. do s.th. (usually bad) **literally** (emphasises the following adjective) **inadequately** insufficiently **Ronan Point** a tower block in east London; at 5.45 am on 16 May 1968 one of the tenants on the eighteenth floor lit her gas oven, causing the explosion which killed five people and injured seventeen. No more tower blocks were built in London after this **to collapse** fall down suddenly

Comprehension

1. Why were politicians and planners so keen to have tower blocks built?
2. What did some people find attractive about the new tower blocks?
3. What three factors made some tower blocks popular with their tenants?
4. What were the two main grievances people had about living in tower blocks?
5. What two choices of action were open to people in the upper floors when the lifts didn't work?
6. Why did it take such a long time for the lifts to be repaired?
7. Why was Doreen Reid so frightened when Tracy didn't answer her call?

Topic work

1. Imagine you live in one of the tower blocks described in the text. Write a letter to Mr Kenneth Campbell, who was chief housing architect for the Greater London Council from 1959 to 1974, the period when most high-rise blocks of flats were built. Explain in your letter why you dislike living in your tower block and what changes should be made.

2. What are the advantages and disadvantages of living in tower blocks? Is there any alternative to building this type of housing?
3. Work in two groups, one consisting of tenants of tower block flats and the other of architects and politicians responsible for the design and construction of tower blocks. Before the two groups have a discussion, the tenants should prepare their questions and comments and the architects and politicians should anticipate what questions might be asked and prepare their defence.

4. High Rise in Peckham – a poem

High Rise in Peckham

High rise flats, towering blocks,
11 – 12 – 14 floors, and more.
Reaching well into the sky
Modern times, people live,
But – is it living?
Cut off from the friendly chat,
Going up into the lift, open the door,
That's that –
High rise flats – the crazy design,
The isolation that becomes a living hell.
Trapped like an animal in a cell.
No contact – oh yes! it's ultra-modern,
But – the loneliness – the high rise flats.
They call it architectural design
Living despair – but of course,
This – is modern times.

P. B. (1980)

Kenneth Baker (ed.), *London Lines*. London: Methuen. p. 145.

Topic work

1. Compare the poem with Doreen Reid's comments about living in a tower block in the previous text.
   What similarities and what differences are there in the two texts?
   What effect do these differences have on the reader?
2. Give your reactions to and comments on the following notes in response to the poem:

'Modern times'	– why 'modern'?
'. . . is it living?'	– why the question? Who's asking the question? And who's supposed to answer?
'living'	– why shouldn't it be living?
'friendly chat'	– where can you have a friendly chat with people nowadays? Why can't you have a friendly chat in a tower block?
'crazy design'	– what is meant by 'crazy'?
'animal'	– what kind of animal? What effect does this have on the animal?
'oh yes! it's ultra-modern'	– 'modern' again – she sounds really pleased to be living there. Is she?
'they'	– who?
'architectural design'	– are these the same people who made the 'crazy design'?
'living despair'	– is this the same as 'living hell'?
'modern times'	– 'modern' again – why?

3. What makes this text a poem? What poetic and non-poetic qualities does it have?
4. Write a poem which expresses what you feel about the house, the block of flats, the street or the area in which you live.

'Muggers kicked the door in on Tuesday night. Police kicked it in again last night looking for them'

Barry Fantoni (1987), *Cartoons*. London: Star Books.

5. The View from Golf Four

I spent the afternoon and evening of 2 January 1982 in Golf Four, the red-striped white Rover that patrols the Stoke Newington area. The driver is Colin Dryden, a burly, bearded Scot. In the passenger seat is his operator, WPC Karen Connor. Our first call is to a 'disturbance' in a row of new council maisonettes just off Stamford Hill. A Cypriot woman in her late fifties, with an orange flowered dress and a red headscarf pulled down to her eyebrows, welcomes Dryden with tears. Her eighteen-year-old son has assaulted her and punched her in the throat. She complains of difficulty in swallowing and speaking. Her English is poor, but the message comes across: 'He hit me, push me. He very bad boy. I bring him up good, why he like this? All the time he want money, but I get only £22 a week, how can I give him? When he was a baby his father hitting me, now he grow up he hitting me too. Why? Why?' She cries out at the injustices of destiny. Dryden has been called here before; this has been going on since the boy was a juvenile. He tells her simply to lock her door, keep her son out, and phone the police if he comes again. The woman is grateful, as much for the comfort of a visit as for the advice. 'Thank you, thank you. I don't like to waste your time. God bless you. Happy New Year.'

The next call is to a burglary in Mount Pleasant Lane, a row of semi-detached private houses looking out at the back over steep lanes leading down to the River Lea, and at the front across some of the most dismal problem estates in Hackney. The resident had left a back window open and a neighbour had seen two men climb out carrying plastic bags. It is a fact of life in Hackney that any way of entry left open will, with a probability approaching unity, be entered, just as surely as scattered breadcrumbs will be lifted by hungry birds.

Golf Four the code name of this patrol car **Stoke Newington** district in north London **burly** strong and heavily built **operator** radio operator **WPC** woman police constable **council** i.e. these houses were built by and owned by the town council **maisonette** [meɪzə'net] a small flat with its own outside entrance **Stamford Hill** a district to the north of Stoke Newington **Cypriot** ['sɪprɪət] a person from Cyprus **to punch** hit with the fist **injustice** unfairness **destiny** G. Schicksal **to go on** happen **juvenile** [dʒu:vənaɪl] teenager **semi-detached house** a house joined to another house to form a pair **dismal** G. düster, schrecklich **estate** *here:* area of houses built by the council, usually housing poorer families **resident** person who lives in a house or town **unity** *here:* certainty

Three abortive but typical 'shouts' follow. A female in a fur coat passing a stolen Access card in Mare Street. An attempted mugging in Stamford Hill, where two youths have been chased off by a group of irate Jews (it is rumoured that they are developing a new approach of aggressive group self-defence). In both cases Golf Four is beaten to it by one of the other three area-cars cruising around Hackney. Glue-sniffers, reported to be causing a disturbance at Malvern House on Stamford Hill Estate, have melted away before we arrive. We continue our routine patrol, heading north for Finsbury Park, where crowds of youths hundreds strong are making their way home on foot from a Spurs-Arsenal fixture. Trouble is expected but does not materialize. Along West Bank Karen Connor points out the locations of three murders in the past year, two of them over arguments at a drinking den in a private house.

On to the major red-light district in Hackney, around Queen's Drive. Most inner-city areas have such market-places in human flesh, where the local female poor sell their wares to passers-through with funds to spare. The location of this one is determined by the proximity of an ample supply of the cheaper kind of hotel and of the major trunk route of Seven Sisters Road. Unfortunately, it is also a residential area. As English law hypocritically allows prostitutes to work, but not to make themselves known, all local females risk being propositioned by kerb-crawlers. Tonight five girls are out 'tomming'. When they spot Golf Four they turn on their heels and walk off briskly. Karen Connor stops three for questioning. They deny they were soliciting. Connor asks if they have any contraceptives in their handbags and takes their word when they say no. There is no need to come heavy: a special police 'tom squad' is operating in the area and already driving the trade away, though only to other streets in Hackney.

abortive without a successful result **shout** *here:* call to a police car **to pass** *here:* use to obtain goods **Access card** a credit card **irate** [aɪˈreɪt] angry **rumoured** said or told but not necessarily true **to beat s.o. to it** do s.th. or reach a place before s.o. else **to cruise** *here:* drive around an area without a special aim **to melt away** disappear quietly **Spurs** nickname for Tottenham Hotspurs **Arsenal** a famous north London football team **fixture** *here:* football match **to materialize** happen **West Bank** a street in Stamford Hill **location** place **proximity** nearness **ample** enough; more than is necessary **trunk route** a main road **residential** consisting of private houses, with no offices or factories **hypocritically** [hɪpəˈkrɪtɪkli] G. heuchlerisch **tomming** (slang) looking for customers **to spot** see **briskly** quickly **to come heavy** use one's authority to the full **tom squad** (slang) group of policemen dealing with prostitutes and their customers

The radio bleeps again. Down in Shoreditch a gang of forty white youths are being chased after a mugging. We race down Kingsland High Street, but by the time we get there most of the culprits have been caught and are stamping, like wild horses in a corral, inside a ring of police. Dryden adjusts his speed according to the urgency of the call: slower for a 'disturbance', which could be anything from a neighbours' quarrel to a mass punch-up; faster, with two-tone horn and blue light, for serious violence, robberies or burglaries where there is a chance of catching the offender on the spot. . . .

The climax of the evening is a call to all units to proceed to Nisbett House in Homerton, where Golf Three is in trouble and has requested assistance. It is a grim tenement of dark, rectangular, walk-up blocks, five storeys high, arranged around a central courtyard. A black man has barricaded himself in his flat. He is standing at a ground-floor window, clutching a baby. Another child is inside. His common-law wife is out in the courtyard; she is nursing a badly injured arm and has a large purple bruise below her left eye. A white neighbour commiserates: 'Was that the row that was going on earlier?' 'He's been beating me up all day, since this morning.' 'I heard it. You could hear the screams all over the court. I saw at least thirty men walk past, and not one of them lifted a finger to help. I thought it was disgusting.' By late evening an exceptionally public-spirited neighbour finally called the police. Golf Three arrived. The wife wanted to prefer charges. When the officers tried to arrest the man, he lunged at them with a knife. They drew their truncheons and he ran into the kitchen and got a meat cleaver. The police retreated with the wife. The man locked them out, with the children still in the bedroom.

When we arrive, other police officers are talking to him through the window. Two white police minis draw up. Four alsatians leap out and pull their handlers along to the grass outside the window, snarling at the man. Another police van – the Immediate Response Unit, introduced after the

to bleep make a high, repeated sound to attract attention **Shoreditch** a district south of Stoke Newington **culprit** a person believed to be guilty of a crime **to adjust** change **punch-up** (slang) fist fight **to proceed to** go to **grim** G. trostlos **tenement** block of flats **rectangular** G. rechteckig **to clutch** hold tightly **common-law wife** a woman considered to be a man's wife because they have lived together for a long period, even though they are not married **bruise** [bru:z] G. Prellung **to commiserate** express sorrow or pity for s.o. **to beat up** wound or injure s.o. very severely by hitting **court** courtyard **to lift a finger** make a small effort **public-spirited** willing to help other people, without thinking of one's own advantage **to prefer charges** G. Klage einreichen **to lunge at s.o.** [lʌndʒ] G. sich auf jmd. stürzen **cleaver** G. Hackbeil **to snarl** make low angry sounds like an animal **van** G. Lieferwagen

1981 riots – screeches to a halt and ten men jump out with riot shields and crash helmets. Residents hang, silhouetted, out of the upper-floor windows. The man under siege begins to cool down a little in the face of such superior force. He agrees to come out peaceably, under protest: 'There's no right for anyone to break into a man's house and beat his head in.' He is led out, complaining, as a short-sleeved policeman holds him firmly by the arm. 'Get back where you came from,' shouts a middle-aged white man in a bobble hat as the captive is loaded into a dark blue van. The children are carried out and brought to the mother, all three of them crying as they are driven off to the station. Father follows, handcuffed, inside the Black Maria.

So much of the inner city's essence was enacted here: two people, both, as it happened, with no work, imprisoned in squalid architecture, loudly destroying each other and their children. Apathy or passive withdrawal among neighbours. And the grand finale, the police acting as undertakers at the public burial of what, once upon a time, must have been a human relationship.

So it went on, pursuing stolen cars, calming angry disputes between a tenant and his resident landlord, between next-door neighbours and at a noisy reggae party. It has been, according to Colin Dryden, a fairly quiet night, with less in the way of serious crime than average. But it has served well as a guided tour of the inner city's sights, its victims and the victims of its victims. For the saddest aspect of such places is the way they accentuate adversity, setting their inhabitants at each other's throats like rats in an overcrowded cage.

Paul Harrison (1983), *Inside the Inner City.* (Penguin Books, 1983) © Paul Harrison, 1983, pp. 33–7.

1981 riots the riots that took place in Brixton, south London, from 10–12 April 1981 (Friday, Saturday, Sunday); no one was killed but 28 buildings were badly damaged or destroyed by fire and on Saturday 279 policemen and 45 members of the public were injured **to screech** make a high sharp sound **under siege** G. belagert; umstellt **bobble hat** G. Bommelmütze **to handcuff** G. Handschellen anlegen **Black Maria** [mər'aɪə] a vehicle used by the police to transport prisoners **to enact** *here:* show; present **squalid** dirty and uncared-for **undertaker** s.o. whose job it is to arrange funerals **burial** ['berɪəl] putting a dead body in the ground **tenant** s.o. who pays rent to use a flat or house **landlord** a person from whom s.o. rents all or part of a building **to accentuate** *here:* make worse **adversity** bad fortune

Comprehension

As none of the answers to the following questions are given explicitly in the excerpt, explain why you give the answer you do:

1. Why did the Cypriot woman have difficulty in swallowing and speaking?
2. What is the explanation for her son's behaviour?
3. Where did the burglars of the house in Mount Pleasant Lane come from?
4. Why should the location of a red-light district be determined by cheap hotels and a major trunk route?
5. Why is it 'unfortunate' that the red-light district is residential?
6. Why was the neighbour at Nisbett House 'exceptionally' public-spirited?
7. What did the middle-aged white man mean when he shouted "Get back where you came from"?
8. What does the writer mean when he writes, "the inner city's ... victims and the victims of its victims"?

Language skills

The writer probably based this part of his book on brief notes he took on the afternoon and evening of 2 January 1982. To make the narrative more vivid it is told partly in the present tense. Reconstruct the notes you think the writer might have made while accompanying Golf Four, but using the past or past perfect tense where appropriate. Compare your notes with those of other students.

Topic work

Work in groups of three or four. Discuss what are the most important types of crime in your home town. Compare them with the crimes described in the text. Choose three crimes committed in your home town and note down any suggestions you can make about how to deal with them.

Now compare your list and suggestions with those of other students. Do they agree with your suggestions for solving the problem? Work together and draw up a common list of proposals.

Organise a class discussion on ways to beat crime in the cities.

6. London Parks

The parks are London's precious feature. Its lungs, Lord Chatham said. Devised for the 'singular comfort' of the monarch, these former hunting grounds remain the property of the Crown, and the most effective emblem of the royal city. They are also a safety valve for the people – where the anarchist stands on his soap box, the city on its ceremony.

When the Mediterranean lends us its sun from the end of May, clothes come off, beer bellies tumble out, and men walk round ridiculously in brown pants, shoes and socks. In the 5,671 acres a Londoner can be at his loneliest or his most gregarious; withdrawn or hung-out – like the 'impeccably dressed bowler-hatted elderly gent' who exposed himself to Susan Hill, the contemporary novelist, close to the Albert Memorial.

For some Londoners the parks exist as an outdoor sports ground; for others as a place to walk – if not bury – the dog. For the majority they are a private garden, and jealously guarded as such. When asked what it would cost to enclose a section of Hyde Park, Sir Robert Walpole told Queen Caroline, 'Only Three Crowns, Madam – those of England, Ireland and Scotland.'

In his *Letters from England*, published in 1923, Karel Capek tells how, when watching a man amble off the path and across the grass, he could not believe his eyes. Looking nervously about him, Capek decided to follow suit. He put one foot tentatively forward, then another. 'Nothing happened,' he exclaimed. 'Never have I had a feeling of such unrestricted liberty as in that moment.' Much of the Londoner's character and view of the

Lord Chatham ['tʃætəm] William Pitt, First Earl of Chatham (1708–1778) **to devise** think up; plan; invent **singular** (arch.) special **to stand on ceremony** insist on c.; consider c. very important **belly** G. Bauch **to tumble out** fall or roll out **pants** *here:* trousers **gregarious** [grɪ'geərɪəs] liking to be in the company of other people **hung-out** (slang) feeling free to do what one likes, without worrying what other people think **impeccably** [ɪm'pekəbli] perfectly **to expose oneself** show one's sexual parts **contemporary** belonging to the present time **the Albert Memorial** memorial to Prince Albert, the husband of Queen Victoria **to enclose** surround with a fence **Karel Capek** ['tʃapek] Czech dramatist and novelist (1890–1938) **to amble** walk slowly **to follow suit** do the same as s.o. else **tentatively** ['tentətɪvli] hesitantly; slowly and carefully **unrestricted** without any limits world, he concluded, was explained by his right to walk across a meadow as if he were a combination of wood nymph and landed proprietor.

'Most Londoners are within reach of a park where they can lose themselves,' says Ken Livingstone, a man who cannot walk down the street without being recognised and stopped. 'In all of them, you can get to a point in the centre where you are completely cut off.' Second only to politics is his love of natural history. 'I often take my nephew and his friends and poke around in ponds. Salamanders and Manchurian toads aren't demanding.'

An early winter morning in Kensington Gardens. Gulls swoop on the Round Pond where Percy Bysshe Shelley sailed his paper boats. Dogs chase leaves hopelessly. A man stands unnaturally still, feeding two squirrels. A woman walks briskly to work, crunching down the Broad Walk between the lime trees.

I cross the Serpentine bridge and head towards Jacob Epstein's statue of Rima. It commemorates the bird woman in *Green Mansions*; also the place where the novel's author, the naturalist W. H. Hudson, slept on first coming to London. A little further on are the red brick offices of London's Central Royal Parks.

From an upstairs room in a hidden building, the young superintendent is marshalling her staff as they prepare for the day's planting, pruning and turfing. Over a cup of tea she decides on Ahmed's application for leave, and on other matters relating to her 187-strong team. She then looks at the letters requesting coach permits; permissions to hold a demonstration, a

wood nymph a goddess in the form of a young girl who lives among the trees **landed proprietor** s.o. who owns a large piece of land **Ken Livingstone** the leader of the Greater London Council – the governing body of London – until its abolition in 1986, now Labour MP for a London constituency **natural history** the study of plants, animals and rocks **to poke around** search; look for s.th. **toad** G. Kröte **demanding** needing a lot of attention or care **Kensington Gardens** a park adjoining to the west of Hyde Park **gull** (also seagull) a large seabird **to swoop** fly downwards suddenly **Percy Bysshe Shelley** English Romantic poet (1792–1822) **squirrel** G. Eichhörnchen **briskly** in a quick and active manner **to crunch** make a crushing noise **lime tree** G. Linde **Serpentine** ['sɜ:pəntaɪn] lake in Hyde Park **Jacob Epstein** (Sir) British sculptor (1880–1959) **Rima** the sculpture, produced in 1925, is a large eagle-like bird; it represents the semi-human embodiment of the spirit of the forest **Green Mansions** a novel written in 1904 **naturalist** a person who studies plants and animals **William Henry Hudson** 1862–1918 **superintendent** *here:* person in charge of the park **to marshall** gather together in the right place **to prune** cut off or shorten the branches of a tree or bush **to turf** G. Grassoden verlegen **application** official request **leave** permission to be absent from work **coach** bus used for excursions or long-distance travel **permit** ['pɜ:mɪt] official written statement giving permission to do s.th.

sponsored walk, a school outing, a veteran car rally. Most are run-of-the-mill, but she is alert for anything that challenges the status quo. Due to their central location her parks are always subject to pressure – from those who want to lay cables, build underground car parks, even tunnels. Patrick Abercrombie's 1943 *Plan* envisaged a tunnel all the way to Whitehall.

Her paperwork done, she goes out. She aims to spend half her time in the open. It is why she wanted the job twenty-one years ago, after a childhood spent on an estate in the City, overlooking a window box. From the age of sixteen, and from Regent's Park to Wandsworth Common, she has dug, forked and hoed a path which has led to her present responsibility for the Central Royal Parks, and the gardens of 10 Downing Street, Clarence House and Buckingham Palace.

Because the system has been built up over decades, much of her job consists of caretaking and maintenance. In the spring she plants the garden beds opposite Buckingham Palace with 40,000 tulips. In the summer, with 14,000 geraniums – the red of a Guardsman's tunic. On state occasions, her staff sweep and clean The Mall. Traditionally, the major occasions happen in Hyde Park, where there has been a gun salute to the monarch since the time of Elizabeth I. With fewer trees and more open space, Hyde Park lends itself to both military events and demonstrations. In 1984 the Campaign for Nuclear Disarmament held a rally for 300,000. Then the major general reviewed the Household Cavalry. Since the increase in fast food, rubbish has become a headache. So too has lead pollution, which damages the trees close to the road.

sponsored walk a walk to raise money for charity in which sponsors pay money for a certain distance walked **outing** excursion **run-of-the-mill** ordinary; not special **alert** watchful **status quo** [steɪtəs kwəʊ] the existing state of affairs **location** situation; position **subject to** G. ausgesetzt **Patrick Abercrombie** (1879–1957) English architect and town planner, he led the team which produced the first plan for Greater London in 1944 **to envisage** [ɪn'vɪzɪdʒ] see as a future possibility **Whitehall** street in London, site of the main government offices and ministries **estate** area of houses and flats built by the council, usually housing poorer families **Regent's Park** park to the north-west of central London **common** area of grassland which everyone is free to use **to hoe** G. hacken **Clarence House** home of the Queen Mother **caretaking** looking after a house and its garden **maintenance** keeping in good condition **state occasion** a state ceremony **The Mall** [mɔ:l] wide road to Buckingham Palace through St. James's Park **gun salute** cannon are fired to show respect for the monarch **to lend itself** be suitable for **Campaign for Nuclear Disarmament** an organisation whose aim is that Great Britain should give up nuclear weapons **to review** inspect **Household Cavalry** the regiments which guard the Royal family **rubbish** waste material that is thrown away

The superintendent lives in a cottage on Hyde Park. One of thirteen such buildings, it is guarded by two ferocious dogs. Previously she lived in Richmond. She saved two hours a day when she moved. It is quiet at night, but if she wants peace on a hot summer's day, she has to leave the parks altogether. At night she can hear the bats, rabbits and cormorants, although the owls seem to have gone. Occasionally, a fox can be seen making its way across the grass. 'It usually gets run over.'

On her walks the superintendent is sometimes asked by tourists if they can tread on the grass. Americans, she says, are surprised it is safe to walk in the parks at all. She talks with affection of the die-hard solitary bird-feeders. Following the same route, they are recognised every morning by the birds and squirrels which come flocking for crumbs.

Recently she has noticed a new trend in the park. It involves young men and women going up to trees. Wrapping their arms around the trunk, they remain there and hug for a few minutes.

Nicholas Shakespeare (1986), *Londoners*. London: © Sidgwick and Jackson. pp. 214–6.

ferocious [fə'rəʊʃəs] very fierce **Richmond** a pleasant suburb in the south-west of London **bat** a flying mouselike animal **cormorant** a type of large black sea-bird **occasionally** sometimes **die-hard** s.o. who refuses to change his habits or ideas **to flock** gather in a large crowd **crumb** tiny piece of bread or cake **to involve** have as a part

Comprehension

1. Who owns London's parks?
2. Why would it have cost her crown if Queen Caroline had tried to enclose Hyde Park?
3. Why was Karel Capek so surprised when he saw a man walking on the grass in a London park?
4. Why did he exclaim that "nothing happened," after walking on the grass himself?
5. Where did W. H. Hudson first sleep when he came to London?
6. Who is Ahmed?
7. What are the advantages and disadvantages for the superintendent of living in Hyde Park?
8. Why are American tourists surprised that it is safe to walk in London parks?

Language skills

1. Explain what the author means when he writes:
   1. "The parks are London's precious feature. Its lungs, . . ." (l. 1)
   2. "They are also a safety valve for the people . . ." (l. 4)
   3. "When the Mediterranean lends us its sun . . ." (l. 6)
   4. ". . . a man who cannot walk down the street without being recognised . . ." (l. 27/28)
   5. ". . . she has dug, forked and hoed a path which has led to her present responsibility . . ." (l. 56/57)
   6. ". . . rubbish has become a headache." (l. 70)
2. In your own words write down as briefly as possible:
   a) what people can do in London's parks.
   b) what the duties of the park superintendent are.

Topic work

The author writes in a humorous and witty manner. Find and explain examples of his humour.

7. Bedsitland

If you look in the local newsagent's shop windows, you will see many postcard advertisements. Amongst the cards offering second-hand furniture or clothing are cards about flats to let or to share. This is where many Londoners begin a long tedious search for accommodation, ranging from the tolerable to dim and dreary basement flats.

The young arrival in London soon finds that the term "bijou residence" can mean a tiny cell, that "pleasant outlook" can mean two trees at the end of a long dark alley.

But London means work, education or fun; there will always be someone in need of this third-rate accommodation. It is often a matter of "mak-

Bedsitland 'bedsit' from bedsitter or bed-sitting room, a room in which you can sleep and live; place where there are lots of bedsits **newsagent's** a shop which sells newspapers and magazines **to let** rent (a house or room) **tedious** tiring and uninteresting **accommodation** a place to live **to range** *here:* G. reichen **tolerable** acceptable **dreary** sad, grey, dull **basement** room below street level **bijou** ['bi:ʒu:] very small and pretty **residence** place to live **alley** ['æli] narrow street between buildings **third-rate** third class, not very good quality ing do" for the time being and looking out for something better. The rent is often way out of proportion to the space and facilities provided, but there is always someone prepared to pay.

The bedsitter – a simple room – is for those who prefer a little independence. But thin partition walls and shoddy conversion work can mean many noisy intrusions from next door. The independence can often mean loneliness. How do you meet anyone else, when they pass in and out of the warrens without a word?

One place offering company of a sort and a little warmth may be the launderette. For those with little money it offers two advantages: enjoying the warmth from the machines (and not the coin-operated electric heater at home) and the chance of a little company. On a cold night you can put your sweater into the drier and wear it immediately for added heat.

The shared flat is an alternative, expecially if money is a problem. It means sharing a kitchen, bath and living space, but also the rent and sometimes food and entertainment.

Every area in London contains flats occupied by two to six or seven people. Many sharers are friends who met in the city and decided to pool accommodation. Some are people who met by advertising in shops or newspapers. The accommodation is almost infinitely varied, as with the bedsitters. Some are centrally located, and have large pleasant rooms. Others are over-crowded, or far from the city centre. The rents are usually high – certainly more so than in any other town in Britain. It is hard to imagine how many of them manage. But for the single person living in London on an average wage, it is often the only way they can ensure a roof over their heads.

Sandra Alfry (1978), *London Life*. Hove: Wayland Ltd. p. 14.

to make do (coll) use s.th. even if it is not exactly what you really wanted **for the time being** for a limited period **to look out for** search for **out of proportion** *here:* too high **facilities** things that make the place comfortable **independence** being free, not living with other people **partition walls** walls which divide a room up into smaller rooms **shoddy** made cheaply and badly **conversion** *here:* changing one room into two or more rooms **intrusion** s.th. which disturbs **warren** ['wɒrən] *here:* place in which usually too many people live; place where rabbits live **launderette** shop where people can wash their clothes in washing machines **sweater** ['swetə] thick pullover made of wool **to pool** share **varied** of different kinds **located** situated **to manage** *here:* live on a small amount of money **to ensure** [ɪnʃʊə] *here:* make certain that you have

Comprehension

1. Why are flats in London so expensive?
2. Why have you got to be careful when looking at the descriptions people give of their flats to let?
3. Why do so many young people go to London?
4. What are the two main disadvantages connected with living in a bedsitter?
5. Why would someone living in a bedsitter go to a launderette?
6. What are the advantages and disadvantages of sharing a flat?
7. How might you find someone to share a flat with you?

Topic work

Imagine you have moved to London to work for a few months. Describe your bedsit accommodation, how you found it, and your feelings when you move in.

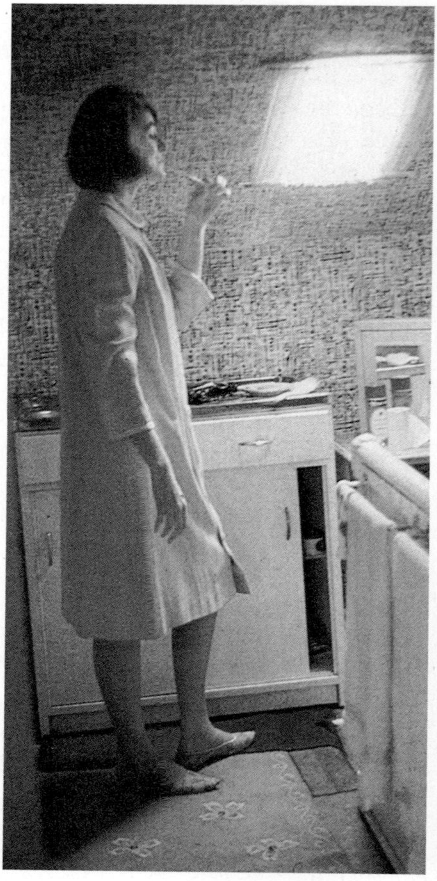

The typical bedsit is one all-purpose room, sometimes dark and dingy, usually impersonal and always cramped. (*London Life*, Wayland Publishers Ltd.)

8. Teargas and Rubber Bullets – a poem

The world turns and twists with rage,
Religious fictions,
Political restrictions,
Vicious new laws,
Political treachery.

They imprisoned you in a concrete wilderness
And threatened you with teargas and rubber bullets.
The architects and politicians
Made millions on the side
In the sixties.

The politicians want you to rot
In the tower block cages.
The police want to fight you with
Teargas and rubber bullets.
They want to frighten you off the streets
They don't want to talk.
They slammed the door in your face.

They want the youths to crawl at their feet
But they won't succeed.
The youths said, No way
And climbed on a wall
Then the bricks started to fall.
It was like a war.

Some people thought the television pictures
Were coming from abroad
And not in their own back yard.
It came as a surprise
To the privileged class
But not to the black working class.

Milton Smalling (1986), *The Battlefield.* London: First Class Publications. pp. 40–1.

teargas ['tɪəgæs] gas used by the police to control crowds **vicious** ['vɪʃəs] cruel, wanting to hurt **treachery** ['tretʃəri] G. Verrat **architect** ['a:kɪtekt] **on the side** dishonestly **tower block** tall block of flats **bullet** ['bʊlɪt] shot fired from a gun **to slam** shut a door making a loud noise **no way** (coll.) (shows strong refusal to do s.th.)

Topic work

1. a) Explain in your own words what you think the poet means by:
   'religious fictions'
   'political restrictions'
   'political treachery'
   b) Who is the 'you' that the poet is addressing?
   c) Who are 'they' in the third and fourth stanzas?
   d) What does the poet mean when he writes:
   'The architects and politicians/Made millions on the side'?
   e) What was 'like a war'?
   f) Why did people think that 'the television pictures/Were coming from abroad'?
   g) Why was what happened not a surprise to the black working class?
2. Identify the formal and structural elements that make the poem a complete whole and give it a sense of continuity.
3. Characterise the tone of the poem. How is this tone created?
4. What judgment of society does the poet seem to be asking us to make?
5. Make notes on your views of modern housing, the police, politicians and, in a class discussion, compare them with those expressed in the poem and with those of your fellow students.

LONDONERS

"To be a Londoner you've got to be first intelligent. And second good-looking. When you're a Londoner, you don't have to think. You know all the answers. Not only do you know what you know. You even know what you don't know."

A speaker at Speaker's Corner, Hyde Park, quoted in Nicholas Shakespeare, *Londoners.*

1. Cockney – the Language of Londoners

The life of the street was crucial to the making of late-Victorian Cockney. The close-knit rural communities of East Anglia, Kent and Middlesex from which the majority of East Enders came kept their oral traditions alive on the streets, and in the ale houses and wash houses of Limehouse and Stratford East. When the rural poor were crammed together in the slums of the East End many of the conditions in which the oral tradition of the countryside had flourished were intensified. There was no privacy; everything happened on the street; they were isolated in a particular part of London, not least by the twists and turns of the River Thames. The tradition of spoken English lives on to this day, as Bob Barltrop puts it:

Cockney a person born and living in London, especially in the East End, the area to the east of the Tower of London; it means literally 'cock's egg' and was originally used contemptuously by country people of ignorant town dwellers **crucial** ['kru:ʃəl] very important **Victorian** belonging to the period in which Queen Victoria reigned (1837–1901) **close-knit** [ˌkləʊs'nɪt] tightly bound together **rural** in the countryside **East Anglia** region in the east of England, consisting of Norfolk, Suffolk and parts of Essex and Cambridgeshire **Kent** county to the south-east of London **Middlesex** county to the west of London, now no longer in existence **ale house** (arch.) place where people meet to drink beer **Limehouse** district in east London **Stratford** district in east London **to cram together** push into a small space **to flourish** ['flʌrɪʃ] G. gedeihen **privacy** ['prɪvəsɪ] **Bob Barltrop** a writer on Cockney culture and language

If there's anything that distinguishes the Cockney, it's his sheer enjoyment of words. He loves to stand them on end and make them jump through hoops and turn circles... There's nothing better to a Cockney than to talk – to talk enjoyably, to talk colourfully, to use wonderful phrases. That's Cockney.

This love of nuance, rhythm, word-play and innovation is part of the explanation for the persistent rule-breaking in some elements of Cockney grammar. Some phrases simply *sound* better when the grammar (strictly speaking) is wrong. "That ain't got nothing to do with it" is much more emphatic than the Standard English "That has nothing to do with it".

What does Cockney sound like? Undoubtedly, it has changed since its Victorian days. Then it was, apparently, thinner and reedier in sound. Older Cockneys still say *gardin* for "garden", *year'oles* for "earholes" and *chimbley* for "chimney". There is a continuity in the pronunciation of *th*, which is often replaced by *f*, as in *barf* for "bath", or by *v*, as in *bruvver* for "brother" or *bovver* for "bother". The related loss to this is the glottal stop, the neglect of the *t* in words like "butter", "bottle", "rotten" which in Cockney can best be represented as *bu!er, bo!le, ro!en.* Similarly, "didn't" becomes *didn* and "haven't" turns into *'avn*. The only alternative to the redundant *t* is *d*, as in *geddoud of i'*, or *you bedder no'*. The characteristic for which Cockney is famous, of course, is the silent *h*. Barltrop points out the dropped *h* has nothing to do with ignorance. He tells the story of the child reading a picture-book with its father. They turn the page and the father says: "That's an 'edgeog. It's really two words. Edge and og. They both start with an aitch."

Then there is a whole class of speech characteristics which betray the rural roots of Cockney. For instance, it is very common to find the *g* missing from *ing* endings like: *eatin'*, and *drinkin'*. This is precisely the speech of Fielding's Squire Western and his heirs in English literature. Even now it is fashionable, in certain parts of the English shires, to talk about *shootin'* or *fishin'*. Similarly, the Cockney pronunciation of "gone", "off" and "cough" (*gorn, of,* and *corf*) is still used by upper-class country speakers without a trace of class shame. The characteristic long *o, oo,* for *ew*, almost certainly originated in East Anglia: so it is no surprise that Cockneys and Americans have a number of pronunciations in common, including the *oo* for *ew*. Cockneys say *stoo* for "stew", *nood* for "nude", *noos* for "news",

sheer absolute **innovation** *here:* new word or use of a word **undoubtedly** [ʌn'daʊtɪdli] without any doubt **reedy** thin and high **glottal stop** G. Knacklaut **redundant** not used or needed **hedgehog** G. Igel **Fielding** Henry Fielding; English novelist and dramatist; author of Tom Jones (1707–1754) **squire** ['skwaɪə] country gentleman, a landowner **the shires** country areas **to originate in** come from just like many Americans. In some respects, Cockney preserves in a vital form uses of English eradicated by education and the drive towards standardization.

Cockneys will drop letters and slur words in many different ways. "Old" becomes *ol'*. "An" becomes *ern*, as in *ern afternoon*. "You", as everyone who has attempted to render Cockney in print knows, is *yer*. The *o* in words like "tomato" and "potato" becomes *er*, as in *barrer* for "barrow". The main shopping street in Hackney, the Narrow Way, is known as the *Narraway*. Words get run together in Cockney. "God help us" becomes *gawdelpus*, and "God blind me" becomes *gorblimey*. Lesser examples like *lotta* for "lot of" pop up in unlikely places. A recent British Milk Marketing Board campaign played on Cockney slang and pronunciation – and an implicit toughness – with the copy-line *Gotta lotta bottle*.

One element of Cockney that has permeated the mainstream of the language is rhyming slang: *a bull and a cow* for "a row", and *Cain and Abel* for "a table". The popular view which holds that Cockney is, essentially, composed of this comes from the music-hall image of the Cockney – the cheeky chappy, with a heart of gold and a joke on his lips, who shows true grit in hard times and knows how to have a party when the day is over. In fact, until the 1930s, the currency of rhyming slang was quite small – Shaw, for instance, never used it. For many Cockneys, it was merely cheerful word play, in which a "suit" became a *whistle and flute*, a "hat" was a *titfer* or *tit-for-tat*, "gloves" were *turtles*, or *turtle-doves* and "boots" were *daisies* or *daisyroots*. Rhyming slang was also used as a form of euphemism: *in the rude* for "nude", and *Bristols* for "breasts" (Bristol City = titty). Some famous examples of rhyming slang also have an undertone of comment – *trouble and strife* (wife), *holy friar* (liar), and *bees and honey* (money). *Rabbit*, which is short for *rabbit and pork* (talk), has now passed into the mainstream of English in the common phrase *rabbiting on*. When the entertainment industry took hold of rhyming slang, however, and put

vital living **to eradicate** destroy completely **drive** planned effort **to slur** pronounce (a word) unclearly **barrow** G. Schubkarre **gorblimey** (slang) an expression of surprise **to pop up** appear, occur **unlikely** improbable, unexpected **Board** an official organisation **to play on** make use of **implicit** understood but not directly expressed **copy-line** slogan; short phrase with an advertising message **bottle** (a pun) a) a glass container; b) courage **to permeate** ['pɜːmɪeɪt] spread or pass into **mainstream** main part of **to hold** believe **music-hall** type of theatre show with songs, humour and special acts **cheeky** G. keck **chappy** fellow **true grit** real courage **currency** use, knowledge of **Shaw** George Bernhard Shaw, Irish dramatist and critic (1856–1950) **euphemism** ['juːfəmɪzm] the use of a more pleasant, less direct word for a word which might offend people it in the mouths of Cockney characters like Alf Garnett and Arthur "Arfur" Daley, it became elevated into a kind of Cockney code. Bob Barltrop is clear about the myth:

Everybody knows about rhyming slang. It's very much overdone. A lot of the slang you hear is just the invention of scriptwriters. By the way, it wasn't confined to Cockneys. In the past all kinds of people used it. One of the characteristics of Cockney is to pick up what other people have thrown away and preserve it.

Despite the overstatement, rhyming slang *does* exist, and is springing up all the time. When Edward Heath was prime minister *heath* became rhyming slang for "teeth", prominent features in the premier's smile. More recently, a *John Selwyn* became rhyming slang for a *bummer*, "a bad situation", after the then chairman of the Conservative Party, John Selwyn Gummer.

Robert McCrum, William Cran, Robert McNeil (1986), *The Story of English*. London: Faber and Faber/BBC Publications. pp. 276–279.

Alf Garnett, Arthur Daley Cockney characters in a television series **to elevate** raise to a high position **to overdo** use too much **script** words spoken by actors in a play **overstatement** making s.th. seem more important than it is

Comprehension

1. In what ways were the conditions of Cockneys in London similar to those of their rural forefathers?
2. Make a list of the sounds which distinguish Cockney from standard English.
3. What pronunciations does Cockney have in common with upper class English?
4. Why do Cockneys and Americans have a number of pronunciations in common?
5. Explain the 'undertone of comment' in the rhyming slang expressions 'trouble and strife', 'holy friar' and 'bees and honey'.
6. Why does the writer refer to the 'myth' of rhyming slang?

Language skills

In this passage the author uses a number of adverbs and adverbial phrases

a) to show that he is expressing a viewpoint, i. e. to tell us about his attitude to what he is saying, and

b) to make a connection with preceding ideas or sentences.

The 'viewpoint' adverbs are: strictly speaking (l. 17/18); undoubtedly (l. 20); apparently (l. 21); of course (l. 30); precisely (l. 37); almost certainly (l. 42/43); essentially (l. 61).

The 'connecting' phrases are: similarly (l. 27, 40); for instance (l. 36, 66); however (l. 75); by the way (l. 80).

1. Explain the viewpoint that is being expressed in the 'viewpoint' adverbs and the connection that is being made in the 'connecting' phrases.
2. Add an appropriate viewpoint adverb or a connecting phrase from the list below to the following passage written by a Londoner, commenting on the use of rhyming slang.

I am (1) .... not much of an expert on Cockney rhyming slang. (2) ...., I have lived in London all my life and can (3) .... say with some truth that I have heard and used a good few of these expressions in my time. (4) .... therefore I have never come across some rhyming slang expressions used by so-called Cockneys in some television series.
(5) .... everyone has heard of 'titfer' (tat) for 'hat' and 'currant bun' for son/sun. And even non-Cockneys sometimes use phrases (6) .... 'brass tacks' for 'facts' and 'use your loaf' (of bread) for 'head' and (7) .... don't even know they're using rhyming slang!
But (8) .... some of the expressions used by Arthur 'Arfer' Daley in his TV series I would (9) .... say that they are inventions of his scriptwriters. Who, (10) ...., has ever heard a real Cockney say 'bacon and eggs' for 'legs' or 'pineapple' for 'chapel'?
(11) .... these TV Cockneys, real Cockneys use rhyming slang sparingly and not every time they open their mouths.

(1) a) however	b) definitely	c) admittedly
(2) a) Naturally	b) Consequently	c) However
(3) a) apparently	b) accordingly	c) undoubtedly
(4) a) Essentially	b) Strictly speaking	c) Surprisingly
(5) a) Of course	b) Firstly	c) Personally
(6) a) except for	b) such as	c) above all
(7) a) probably	b) fortunately	c) similarly
(8) a) as regards	b) in addition to	c) like
(9) a) in some respects	b) definitely	c) in conclusion
(10) a) apparently	b) as a general rule	c) for instance
(11) a) In contrast to	b) As regards	c) Like

Topic work

Write a talk to give to the rest of the class agreeing or disagreeing with the statement that "There is no longer any place in a modern society for urban or regional accents and dialects."

2. The Promised Land

In June 1948 hundreds of Jamaicans were invited to a civic tea with the Mayor of Brixton and were afterwards introduced to local dignitaries. They had recently arrived on the *SS Empire Windrush* and the account of their coming to the capital was headlined in the *Evening Standard* 'WELCOME HOME'. These were the first black immigrants to come to London from the New Commonwealth in the post-war years. Many of them were ex-servicemen and they came decked out in their 'Sunday best' suits and jaunty hats. Like the later immigrants who followed them they were poor and had to save hard to buy a one-way ticket. Nevertheless, they had high hopes for the future and were determined to begin by making a good impression. London to them was the promised land, a land of much greater opportunity than the one they had come from. The uniquely friendly welcome they received was in part a recognition of the great contribution made by the Commonwealth and Empire to the Allied victory in the Second World War.

Their arrival began a new era in London's post-war history which would transform the capital into a truly multi-ethnic city. Of course, immigration to London was nothing new. Over the centuries it had attracted many poverty-stricken and persecuted peoples. Huguenots from France; Jews from Eastern Europe and Russia; and the Irish. What was distinctive about this latest wave of immigration was the fact that much of it came from the new Commonwealth, drawing in people whose colour and culture was quite different to most Londoners. In the next fifteen years the pioneer Jamaicans on the *Empire Windrush* were to be followed by almost a quarter of a million more immigrants from former colonies and dependencies in the Caribbean, Asia and the Mediterranean. . . .

Brixton district in south London which forms part of the London Borough of Lambeth **SS** steamship **Evening Standard** a London newspaper **New Commonwealth** the countries which became members of the Commonwealth after the Second World War, in other words all the countries of the Commonwealth apart from Australia, New Zealand and Canada, the most important of which are: Pakistan, Bangladesh, India, Sri Lanka, Nigeria, Ghana, Zambia, Kenya, Uganda, Malawi, Tanzania, Gambia, Sierra Leone, Jamaica, Trinidad and Tobago, the Bahamas, Barbados, Guyana, Malaysia, Singapore, Cyprus, and Malta **ex-serviceman** s.o. who served in the armed forces **jaunty** G. flott, kess **uniquely** *here:* unusually **contribution** help **Huguenots** ['hju:gənɒts] French protestants who left France in the 16th and 17th centuries **Caribbean** [kærɪ'bi:ən]

Within three weeks all of the 492 Jamaicans who had arrived on the *Empire Windrush* had jobs, most typically as electricians, plumbers, coach builders, labourers and clerical workers. Hundreds of professionally qualified immigrants, particularly Asians, found employment in London as doctors and teachers. Although many had to be content with unskilled and unpleasant work that whites didn't want, they were at least able to find a job of some sort. And the drudgery endured by West Indian street sweepers, Asian factory shift workers and Cypriot kitchen hands, was made less painful by the fact that they were earning almost double the wage they would have received in a similar job at home.

They also found accommodation without too much difficulty. One of the most important considerations affecting their choice of where to live was the need to be close to their new jobs. Since many of them worked fairly long hours in what by British standards were not particularly well-paid jobs, a time-consuming and expensive journey was out of the question. The areas where immigrants got their first job were thus likely to develop as ethnic settlements. In the case of Jamaicans it was to be South-West London, expecially Brixton. This was due to the chance fact that Jamaican immigrants in the late 1940s were housed in the old air raid shelters at Clapham, and then directed to South London employment agencies to find work and accommodation. Similarly, the Asian settlement in Southall from the early 1950s onwards began because the personnel manager of Woolfe's rubber factory in the town had been a police officer in the Punjab area of India, and he gave many Punjabi immigrants a job there.

Steve Humphries and John Taylor (1986), *The Making of Modern London 1945–1985*. London: London Weekend Television.

plumber ['plʌmə] s.o. who fits and repairs water pipes and bathroom appliances **coach builder** skilled worker who builds the bodies of motor vehicles and railway carriages **clerical worker** s.o. who works in an office **content** [kən'tent] **shift** period of time worked by a group of workers who are then followed by another group of workers **Cypriot** ['sɪprɪət] s.o. who comes from the island of Cyprus [saɪprəs] **consideration** s.th. to be considered **ethnic** of a racial or cultural group **personnel** [pɜ:sə'nel] **Punjab** ['pʌndʒɑ:b] region in NW India

Comprehension

Decide what evidence there is in the passage for the following statements. If there is no evidence, explain what the passage actually says.

1. The Jamaicans on the *Empire Windrush* were given such a friendly welcome because some of them had been soldiers in the Second World War.
2. The newspaper headline 'WELCOME HOME' indicated that some of the Jamaicans had lived in England before.
3. The Jamaican immigrants bought one-way tickets because they were too poor to afford a return ticket.
4. Londoners had never before experienced immigration in such huge numbers.
5. In comparison with their home countries most immigrants were earning good wages.
6. Immigrants had to live near where they worked because they could not afford long journeys on public transport.
7. The examples of where Jamaicans and Indians lived and worked in London showed that immigrants like to live together in the same area.

Language skills

Find words or phrases in the text which correspond to the following definitions:

(Paragraph 1)

a) put on by the town or city
b) important people
c) dressed in

(Paragraphs 2 and 3)

d) with people of many different cultures and races
e) extremely poor
f) with training only available for well-educated people
g) not needing special training
h) hard, uninteresting work
i) workers

(Paragraph 4)

j) attack by enemy aircraft
k) dealing with the employees of a company

Topic work

Imagine you were one of the Jamaican immigrants who arrived in Britain on the *Empire Windrush* in June 1948. Write a letter home to your relatives describing your feelings and experiences in the first few weeks in London.

3. 'When I'm an MP'

'If you're black you're bound to want to change things,' says Diane Abbott, recently selected as Labour candidate for Hackney North and almost certain to become Britain's first black woman MP at the next General Election. Val Hennessy meets the woman who describes herself as a 'working-class Paddington girl made good'.

Barring sudden death, the end of the world, or victory for the Social Democrats, Diane Abbott will become Britain's first black woman MP at the next General Election. Selected in December [1985] as Labour candidate for Hackney North, a seat with an 8,000 Labour majority, 32-year-old Ms Abbott says she is jubilant to be blazing a trail into the House of Commons.

And what a trail. Mr Speaker will certainly be kept on his toes when the volatile Ms Abbott, whose conversation is peppered with expletives, eventually takes her seat. 'The Commons is a ..... appalling place really, isn't it?' she says, seated at her chaotic desk in the Soho Square office where she works as equality officer for the film and broadcasting union, ACTT.

'It's full of men lounging about in bars all day. Awful baggy grey men in awful baggy grey suits, full of booze and their own importance. Obviously when I'm an MP I'll go along there to speak, but what I'm really looking forward to is the grass roots, getting out among the working people of Hackney.'

bound to having a duty to do s.th. **Hackney** district in north London **Paddington** district in west London **barring** excluding **Ms** [mɪz] a title for a woman who does not want to be called Mrs or Miss **jubilant** filled with great joy **Mr Speaker** the person who controls business in the House of Commons **volatile** ['vɒlətaɪl] quickly becoming angry or dangerous **expletive** word used to express violent feelings **the Commons** the House of Commons **appalling** [ə'pɔ:lɪŋ] very bad **equality officer** employee who makes sure that all employees are treated equally **ACTT** Association of Cinematograph, Television and Allied Technicians **to lounge about** [laʊndʒ] spend one's time in a lazy way, doing nothing **baggy** loose, not tight **booze** (slang) alcoholic drink **grass roots** ordinary people

Diane Abbott with parents and children

Ms Abbott is not one to mince her words. Neither is she one to take to heart the accusations of 'infiltration' and 'vote switching' emanating, for the most part, from Mr Ernie Roberts, the veteran Labour MP she ousted. 'Without wanting to be horrible to Ernie it's obvious that the people of Hackney were fed up with having a 73-year-old white man as their MP.

'Since 1951 the number of black voters in the constituency has increased from 70 people to over 50 per cent of the population. By selecting me the next election will be really exciting because the constituents will say, "Hey, man, we've got the chance to get the first black woman MP into Parliament. It's a historic vote; let's get down to that polling booth." I know how excited the people will be. They're buzzing already.'

Ms Abbott points out that two more safe seats and three marginals are fielding black candidates at the next election. It's about time, she says. All power to British black elbows. She laughs. She slaps her

infiltration *here:* getting into an organisation secretly **vote switching** *here:* changing the way people vote **to emanate from** come (out) from **to oust** [aʊst] force s.o. out and take his position **constituency** an area which elects an MP **polling booth** place where s.o. can mark his voting paper **safe seat** a constituency in which the other party is unlikely to win **marginal** ['ma:dʒɪnəl] a marginal seat: a constituency in which the result is not certain **to field** *here:* enter the competition to become an MP thighs. A sheaf of documents showers unheeded from her desk. Among them are several newspaper cuttings in which she is described as 'left wing', 'a police hater', 'a Scargillite' and 'a race and class warrior'.

Noting the direction of my glance, Ms Abbott rolls her eyes and exclaims: 'I don't let a bunch of right wing ..... worry me. If you let personal attacks get to you then you shouldn't be in politics. The only explanation for these vitriolic press items is that the ..... who write them find the notion of an independent, articulate, young black woman unbelievably threatening, right?

'Of course I'm left wing. If you're black you're bound to want to change things. Unfortunately, in certain narrow minds "black" and "extremist" seem to go together. My politics are no different from Margaret Beckett's or Jo Richardson's [both Labour MPs]. On lots of issues my views are similar to Harriet Harman's, yet these white women don't get slagged off all the time like I do.

'Hassles? I've had hassles all my life. But I can handle it. Life is one perpetual hassle when you're a British black woman.

'When I was up at Cambridge certain people assumed I was there as some sort of token, some sort of charity student scraped up off a Brixton playground and allowed in as a treat. I wanted to say to these patronising ..... "Listen, I have ten 'O' levels, four 'A' levels and no one's ever done me any ..... favours, right?"

'Later, when I worked in TV current affairs, I had to fight to be taken seriously. Even though I was a Cambridge history graduate people were thrown by the fact that I actually had something to say. They'd look at me as if they were thinking, "Who is this black person who's come out from behind a tea trolley?" My experience is that as a woman you always have to be better than a man to get on in life. As a black woman you have to be better still.'

thigh [θaɪ] top part of the leg **sheaf** bundle **unheeded** unnoticed **Scargillite** supporter of Arthur Scargill, the militant leader of the miners' union **vitriolic** [vɪtrɪˈɒlɪk] cruel **item** *here:* article **notion** idea **articulate** able to express thoughts and ideas clearly and effectively **Harriet Harman** a woman Labour MP **perpetual** continual **Cambridge** *here:* Cambridge University **token** *here:* one person who represents a larger group **Brixton** district in south London, part of the London Borough of Lambeth, which has a large number of black residents **'O' levels** GCE 'O' (Ordinary) level, examinations taken by pupils at the age of 16 **'A' levels** GCE 'A' (Advanced) level, examinations taken by pupils at the age of 18 **current affairs** news about political events **graduate** s.o. who has a first degree from a university **trolley** small table on very small wheels

Her late father, she adds, was a welder. Her mother, an ex-hospital worker, now lives in Yorkshire. Her mother's front-room is like a shrine. The walls are hung with school snaps of the young Diane, her exam certificates, press cuttings, school reports, and portraits taken on graduation day. With a laugh, Ms Abbott reveals that her mother sent copies of the graduation photograph overseas to all her relatives who see her as a shining example.

She continues reminiscing: 'I was born in Paddington. I still live there. I'm a working-class Paddington girl made good. When I was eight my family moved to Harrow. It was weird there as we were the only black people. At Harrow County Grammar School I was the only black girl.

'I was a pain; a real tearaway. It was when I came down from Cambridge that I got seriously into politics and joined the Labour Party. I went on to Westminster Council and became involved in women's issues. I worked with the Women's Centre, sorting out hassles with Social Security, crappy housing, single parents' problems.

'It was a bit like being a social worker and was a very good antidote to my TV work. [She worked as a journalist for Thames Television and TV-am.] Television is a very candyfloss world and my council work kept me in touch with reality.'

A former colleague who worked with her at TV-am says: 'You'll hear people say that she's pushy, tough and difficult in negotiations, but she's wonderful, just wonderful, to people on whose behalf she is negotiating.'

Ms Abbott insists that there is more to her life than politics. 'Some people think that if you're a political activist you're at it all the time, always in meetings, at demos, campaigning.' When she's not working she enjoys listening to American soul and reggae music. Bob Marley is her favourite.

She likes reading, too, but is unable to name any favourite authors on the spur of the moment. She's not in the least domesticated and she has no ambition to marry. Buying a house today strikes her as a much more crucial commitment.

The most magical moment of Ms Abbott's life was her first visit to

late who has died recently **welder** s.o. whose job is to join metal by melting **shrine** holy place **snaps** photos **graduation day** day on which a student receives a university degree **to reminisce** [remɪˈnɪs] think about the past **Harrow** a west London suburb **to come down from** *here:* leave **issues** questions; matters **to sort out** solve **Social Security** the Department of Social Security; the government department that deals with money for people who are unemployed, ill or on low incomes **antidote** *here:* G. Gegengewicht **pushy** determined to get things done and succeed **on behalf of** for **to strike s.o.** G. jdm. vorkommen **crucial** [ˈkruːʃəl] very important **commitment** responsibility

Jamaica at the age of 21, not 'making love to a naked man in a Cotswolds hayfield', as has been widely reported. That remark, she insists, was flippantly made in response to an out-of-the-blue phone call from a magazine. At the time, the girls in the office warned: 'You'll live to regret that remark, Diane.' She says she sure has, even though it wasn't entirely made up. After all, she lists romance as one of her interests outside politics.

The Mail on Sunday, 'You' Magazine, 26 January 1986.

Diane Abbott became MP for Hackney North at the 1987 General Election

Cotswolds hills in SW England **flippant** amusing and light-hearted but concerning a serious subject

Comprehension

Write a brief outline of Ms Abbott's life, giving the main events in chronological order. The following notes and questions are a guideline:

- where was she born?
- parents' jobs?
- moved to?
- schools?
- educational qualifications?
- university?
- first job?
- other Jobs?

Language skills

There are a large number of colloquial and slang expressions in the passage. After looking carefully at the context match the meanings below with these expressions:

a) 'made good' (from the headline 5)
b) 'blazing a trail' (l. 15/16)
c) 'is peppered with' (l. 20)
d) 'mince her words' (l. 38/39)
e) 'take to heart' (l. 40)
f) 'fed up with' (l. 47)
g) 'buzzing' (l. 61)
h) 'slagged off' (l. 97)
i) 'Hassles? I've had hassles' (l. 99)
j) 'scraped up off' (l. 106)
k) 'thrown' (l. 117)
l) 'a pain, a real tearaway.' (l. 149)
m) 'crappy' (l. 157)
n) 'candyfloss' (l. 164)
o) 'on the spur of the moment.' (l. 185)
p) 'out-of-the-blue' (l. 197)

1) talking excitedly
2) with no serious thoughts or ideas
3) leading the way in a new development
4) found by chance
5) completely unexpected
6) someone who causes a lot of trouble
7) talk carefully not using unpleasant words
8) be successful
9) without preparation or planning
10) difficult situations
11) very bad
12) frequently includes
13) confused
14) feel the effect of s.th. deeply
15) criticised in a cruel way
16) unhappy with

Topic work

1. Write a brief description of Ms Abbott's character. Get your information from what she says and does, from what other people say about her and from the writer's description of her.
2. "What I would do if I were an MP"
   Write a short speech to convince your fellow students that you would be an ideal candidate for Parliament.

4. A Man Who Earns £11,000 an Hour

The Duke of Westminster owns Mayfair.

Eight o'clock on a wet Monday morning at Heathrow Airport, and the man who has been burdened throughout life with the bitter-sweet soubriquet "the richest man in Britain" is dashing to Terminal One with wife and suitcases in tow, having been luxuriously but incorrectly decanted by a chauffeur at Terminal Two.

He is furious at this unaccustomed inconvenience, although fellow passengers would not guess it as the couple are ushered smiling self-consciously, VIP-style, into their seats before anyone else. During the flight he reads *The Times*, a newspaper which he thinks is so bad that he will not allow it in any of his homes. His wife glances through a fashion magazine and contemplates the day of intense activity ahead.

Gerald Cavendish Grosvenor, sixth Duke of Westminster, Marquess of Westminster, Earl Grosvenor, Viscount Belgrave, Baron Grosvenor (and Captain West-

Mayfair fashionable district in west central London **Heathrow Airport** London's main airport, located on the south-west edge of London **soubriquet** [səʊ'brɪkeɪ] an unofficial name **in tow** [təʊ] following closely behind **decanted** [dɪ'kæntɪd] *here:* let out of his car **unaccustomed** not usual **inconvenience** trouble **to usher** ['ʌʃə] show the way **self-conscious** embarrassed, feeling uncomfortable **VIP** [vi:aɪ'pi:] Very Important Person **Grosvenor** ['grəʊvnə] **Marquess** nobleman ranking between a duke and an earl **Viscount** ['vaɪkaʊnt] nobleman ranking between an earl and a baron **Baron** the lowest ranking nobleman minster to his mates in the Territorial Army) is travelling with the Duchess to Guernsey for the annual general meeting of the local branch of the National Society for the Prevention of Cruelty to Children – an organisation for which he has vowed to raise £12 m in this, its centenary, year. "If you really want a good cure for a hangover, you should wake up one morning with that sort of commitment", he says.

He is a tall man, 32 years old, and chain smokes. He has a slightly haunted look in his dark-circled eyes which occasionally makes him seem older than his years. He is amiable and laughs a lot, bending backwards as he does so. The Duchess Natalia ("Tally") is also tall – nearly six feet – and she has the bearing and shy mischievousness of her friend the Princess of Wales, to whose son, William, she is godmother. Also like the Princess, she married early: in 1978, when she was 19, and a year before her husband succeeded to his title. "I'd much rather start young", she said. "Then I can be taught the proper way to do things, rather than being too set and rigid".

At Harrow, where he passed only two O-levels, Gerald demonstrated that intellectual and financial legacies are not always compatible ("He was very disappointed about his exam results. We weren't. We worried about what sort of chap he would be", says his mother), and he left at 18 to work as a cowboy on a ranch in British Columbia and then as a jackeroo – a trainee farm manager – in New Zealand.

When he returned to England he was employed by an estate agent and a nature conservancy agency before joining the family business at 21, when his father had a stroke which incapacitated him. "Looking back, his death was certainly the most impressionable part of one's life. It was a dreadfully sad time, but because he had been ill for so

Territorial Army reserve army **Guernsey** ['gɜ:nzɪ] second largest of the Channel Islands **to vow** [vaʊ] swear or declare **centenary** [sen'ti:nərɪ] *here:* the year 100 years after its foundation **commitment** promise to do s.th. **haunted** *here:* worried **amiable** ['eɪmɪəbəl] pleasant, friendly **bearing** ['beərɪŋ] the way a person holds their body **mischievousness** ['mɪstʃəvəsnɪs] G. Verschmitztheit **Princess of Wales** the wife of Prince Charles **godmother** G. Patin **to succeed to a title** take the title when the father dies **set** not changing, not flexible **Harrow** exclusive private school in the west London suburb of Harrow **'O' levels** GCE 'O' (Ordinary) levels, examinations taken by pupils at the age of 16 **legacy** s.th. passed on by s.o. **to be compatible** *here:* can exist together in the same person **chap** fellow **British Columbia** a province of Canada, on the Pacific coast **estate agent** s.o. who buys and sells land and houses **nature conservancy agency** an official organisation which tries to protect the natural environment **stroke** G. Schlaganfall **to incapacitate** [ɪnkə'pæsɪteɪt] make s.o. unable to move or be active **impressionable** *here:* making an impression on s.o.

long it was also a time of release and relief for him.

"Over a period of three days my mother, myself and my two sisters were with him continuously. He was at peace with himself, having had a dreadful time. And I recall very well that he suddenly sat up in bed and for the first time in five years spoke with absolute clarity – without a single stutter, and without that mixing-up of words which a stroke gives. He spoke to me and said, 'Look after the girls'. Those were his last words."

The Westminsters are second only to the royal family in the extent of their world-wide property holdings. They have 200 acres in Belgravia, 100 acres in Mayfair, a 1,000-acre sheep farm near Wagga Wagga in Australia, office blocks in Melbourne, 900 acres in Shropshire, 14,000 acres in North Wales, an estate in County Fermanagh (where Viola, Duchess of Westminster, lives), a 20,000 acre estate at Abbeystead, Lancashire ("my switch-off place", says His Grace), the 11,000 acre Eaton Estate in Cheshire, as well as other property developments in Britain, Hawaii, Canada and North America.

There are various estimates of how much all this is worth – most frequently it is said to be about £2,000 m, giving the Duke a useful income of £11,000 an hour. Says Jimmy James, who has been the astute executive trustee of the Grosvenor Estates since 1961, "We don't compete in the figures game, because it is a slightly pointless exercise. Most of the ones I read are gross over-estimates."

release being set free **relief** feeling of comfort after the ending of pain **stutter** difficulty in producing sounds when speaking **extent** area **Belgravia** fashionable residential district in west central London, near Belgrave Square **acre** ['eɪkə] a unit for measuring area; 1 hectare = 2,471 acres **Melbourne** ['melbən] port in SE Australia, capital of Victoria **Shropshire** ['ʃrɒpʃə] county in west central England, now called Salop **estate** large piece of land with one owner **County Fermanagh** [fɜ:'mænə] county in SW Northern Ireland **Lancashire** county in NW England **switch-off place** place where he can relax **His/Her Grace** title used for addressing a Duke or Duchess **Cheshire** ['tʃeʃə] county in NW England **estimate** calculation of the value of s.th. **astute** [ə'stju:t] clever **executive trustee** s.o. who controls property and money for s.o. else **pointless** useless, not having any result **gross** [grəʊs] *here:* completely wrong

Comprehension

1. Why do you think the writer describes the title 'the richest man in Britain' as 'bitter-sweet'?
2. Why does the writer describe the inconvenience the Duke of Westminster suffers at the airport as 'unaccustomed'?
3. Why are the Duke of Westminster and his wife smiling 'self-consciously' when they take their seats in the aeroplane?
4. Why should the commitment to raise £12 m for the National Society for the Prevention of Cruelty to Children be 'a good cure for a hangover'?
5. What does the writer mean when he writes that Gerald demonstrated that 'intellectual and financial legacies are not always compatible.'
6. Why should Jimmy James think that the figures game – estimating the value of the Duke of Westminster's estate – is a pointless exercise?

Topic work

1. Compare the life of the Duke of Westminster with that of the 'Little Beggars' in text II.2 and the residents of the tower blocks in text II.3. Discuss in small groups what could or should be done to reduce such wide discrepancies of wealth and income.
   After these group discussions hold a class debate on the motion: That the property held by the Duke of Westminster should be taken into public ownership for the benefit of the whole community.
2. You have just inherited a legacy worth £1 m. What would you do with this money and how would your life be affected by it? Give a detailed account of what you would do and how you would live.

5. The True Londoner

The true Londoner is probably neither a cockney nor a cauliflower, but the man who tells you his life story in a pub without telling you his name; a presence as solid and familiar, yet ultimately as evanescent as his city. Given London's propensity for fiction and myth, the truest Londoner of all is probably a writer. 'Shakespeare wrote nothing but doggerel lampoon before he came to London,' said Oscar Wilde. 'And never penned a line after he left.'

V. S. Pritchett goes further: 'Most literature was written in London.'

He lives off Regent's Park on what used to be the fearful no-man's-land between London and the farmlands. Historically, all the railway rubbish ended up here. Then it became renowned as the place where Dickens got rid of his wife, installing her with a large allowance in an area that was deemed out of the swim but respectable. Irish navvies and Mrs Dickens gave way to the Greeks. Finally came the intelligentsia.

Short-story writer, novelist, man of letters, critic, the author in 1962 of *London Perceived*, Sir Victor Swadon Pritchett is a link with this past.

'I was born in nineteen hundred,' he says. He is small, tidily dressed in tweed, with a face like well-polished leather – the material of his first trade. 'You would imagine I thought the nineteenth century behind me. I don't. It lasted till the First World War. I remember, as a boy at school, my first public ride on a horse-drawn tram from London Bridge to Tower Bridge.

cauliflower G. Blumenkohl; the French writer Hippolyte Taine (1828–1893) is supposed to have said that a typical Londoner had the face of a prize cauliflower **ultimately** in the end **evanescent** [evəˈnesənt] soon disappearing and forgotten **propensity** [prəˈpensətɪ] a natural tendency to a certain sort of behaviour **doggerel lampoon** G. Schmähschrift in Knittelvers **to pen** write **Regent's Park** park in the north-west of London **fearful** very bad **railway rubbish** *here:* the workers who had constructed the railways **to end up** be in the end **renowned** [rɪˈnaʊnd] famous **Dickens** Charles Dickens (1812–70), English novelist, famous for his humour and criticism of social injustice **to get rid of** G. loswerden **to install s.o.** *here:* give s.o. a place to live **allowance** a regular sum of money **deemed** (arch.) considered, thought **out of the swim** unfashionable, not for people of a high social position **respectable** socially acceptable **navvy** worker employed in the building and construction industries; originally 'navigator', a worker who was employed to dig canals **to give way to** G. verdrängt werden durch **tidily** [ˈtaɪdɪlɪ] G. ordentlich **trade** G. Handwerk

In a glowing moment, my father would take me on a hansom cab. The streets would be packed with horse-drawn traffic. They stank of horse manure, urine and human sweat. In the smarter quarters you could smell scent.

'London was dirty, awfully dirty. It was filthy in fact. Coal smoke from the railways poisoned the sky. You had to have a bath every day, scrubbing hard to remove the grime. It was bad for chests. Coal smoke made everyone cough themselves silly. My life was despaired of when I was a child.

'The weather has greatly improved; so, with industrialisation, have the clothes. You don't see ragged children running barefoot. Yet now people wear untidy, sporty clothes on a Sunday, as opposed to their best. As for punks, a punk strikes me as someone who wants to appear as one of the needy poor. Immediately I see a shaven head, I think, Oh God, lice in the family.

'The poor were feared collectively as a domestic terror. People had a catastrophic dread of them. My fears now are quite precise. They're about being mugged or having a bag snatched. There are ten cases a day in Harrods, I was told. It's incredible that one should feel afraid to walk anywhere now. In my youth, London was a tough city, but it had very little crime. It was more characterised by fights. I remember women fighting with each other drunkenly outside a pub, watched by the crowd.

'Old London was dictated by old middle-class virtues and vices – solid respectability, a feeling you were better than your neighbours, prudency and decency, consideration to your own class, not to any outside it.

'My father, if he came back today, would like the shops enormously. But he would expect to go about and be respected and deferred to. Though his life was modest, in his own job he had a certain position.

hansom cab two-wheeled horse-drawn carriage used as a taxi until the beginning of the 20th century **manure** waste matter from animals **smart** fashionable **scent** perfume **filthy** very dirty **to scrub** rub with a hard brush to get clean **grime** thick black dirt **to despair of s.o.'s life** lose all hope that s.o. will live **ragged** ['rægɪd] dressed in old torn clothes **barefoot** without any shoes on **to strike me as** have the same effect on me as **needy** without food and clothing **lice** G. Läuse **domestic** *here:* G. einheimisch **to have a dread of s.o.** be very afraid of s.o. **to mug** rob (usually violently and in a public place) **Harrods** probably the world's most famous shop, situated in Knightsbridge and founded by Henry Charles Harrod in 1849 **vice** evil behaviour; opposite of 'virtue' **prudency** being careful before taking any action; not taking any risks **decency** always acting in a socially acceptable way; not doing anything shocking **consideration** G. Rücksicht **to be deferred to** be shown respect because of one's superior social position

'He would notice the vast population from Asia and India. Before the War they were an eccentricity. People were fond of the solitary black or the solitary Chinaman. Now they walk in crowds among us.

'He would notice in the little boutiques – which I find infuriating – the reproductions which hung on his wall. I remember one called *Wedded.* It had a Roman with a tiger skin walking along a castle wall with his lady. It made me laugh. Ten years ago I was given one as a present. Now it's an *objet trouvé.*

'He would notice how high London has become. Like Venice, London was a low city. When I came to this area in the fifties and walked to the top of Primrose Hill, I looked down on a flat-roofed forest because there were so many trees. The only high building was a spire. Now it's difficult to see St Paul's.

'It remains, though, a very hospitable city – a very affectionate city to strangers. A familiar city, and a very hypocritical one. I love the English hypocrisy of going to market and being called Dear and Darling and Ducks, knowing perfectly well you're not dear nor darling nor ducks. But Londoners like these customs, and the way it's always been done. If we can help it, we don't forget the past in the present.

'In their imaginations, the Victorians were never in London. Their imaginative life was outside, abroad. They wanted London to be in Rome. Now the middle classes want to be in Spain or the Bahamas, glamorously going off to places others cannot get to. Geographical heroes. East Enders are different. They're peculiar to themselves, like an extra nation. In the East End there's a hero in every street.

'That's really the secret to London, the key. It's a place where people are allowed to develop their character to a unique degree. I was in Hampstead not so long ago, rounding a corner, when I came upon two middle-aged men who had just bumped into each other. They were glad to meet again.

infuriating making you very angry **skin** G. Fell **objet trouvé** any ordinary object considered from an aesthetic viewpoint **Primrose Hill** hill to the north of Regent's Park **spire** pointed top of a church tower **hospitable** friendly to strangers **affectionate** showing that you like or love s.o. **hypocritical** [ˌhɪpəˈkrɪtɪkəl] talking or acting in an insincere way; not really meaning what you say **Dear, Darling, Ducks** friendly ways of addressing s.o. whose name you don't know **glamorously** doing s.th. in an exciting and attractive way **East Ender** s.o. who lives in the East End of London, the area to the east of the Tower of London **unique** [ju:ˈni:k] which doesn't exist anywhere else **Hampstead** district in north-west London **to bump into s.o.** meet s.o. by chance

'"Where've you been?" said one.

'"Bosham," the other replied.

'"Bosham! Heavens, do you know Bosham?" said the other.

'"Bosham. Of course I know Bosham. I'm a well-known character there."'

'This is what a Londoner wants to be, a character. One who is known for something off-duty, something peculiar, yet something which makes him belong to a set – like people who only go to one pub. It is a conceit. We have a lot of conceit, but we are devoid of vanity.

'I don't think I'd want to live anywhere else,' he said.

Nicholas Shakespeare (1986), *Londoners*. London: © Sidgwick and Jackson. pp. 34–37.

Bosham ['bɒzəm] small town in Sussex **off-duty** *here:* unusual **set** group **conceit** [kən'si:t] *here:* behaviour special to one person; thinking you are a special person **to be devoid of** have no **vanity** thinking too highly of yourself

Comprehension

1. What are the main characteristics of the 'true' Londoner mentioned in this passage?
2. What does this passage tell you about V. S. Pritchett?
3. What are the main differences between the London of V. S. Pritchett's childhood and today?

Language skills

Explain in your own words what the author means by the following expressions:

1. '... where Dickens got rid of his wife ...' (l. 11/12)
2. 'In a glowing moment ...' (l. 22)
3. '... made everyone cough themselves silly.' (l. 28/29)
4. 'The poor were feared collectively as a domestic terror.' (l. 36)
5. '... in his own job he had a certain position.' (l. 48)
6. '... there's a hero in every street.' (l. 73)
7. 'We have a lot of conceit, but we are devoid of vanity.' (l. 85/86)

Topic work

V. S. Pritchett said of London: "I don't think I'd want to live anywhere else." Could you say that of your home town? Write a short report giving the reasons why you would or would not want to live anywhere else and then discuss your opinions in class.

6. An Absolute Beginner

'Hullo, Jules,' I said to him. 'And how's my favourite yobbo?'

'Don't call me Jules,' he said. 'I've already told you.'

Which he has – perhaps 200,000 times or so, ever since I invented the name for him, on account of Vernon = Verne = Jules of *Round the World in Eighty Days.*

'And what are you doing in my darkroom, Julie?' I asked this oafo brother of mine.

He'd got up off the camp bed in the corner – all blankets and no sheets, just like my Vernon – and came over and did an act he's done with monotonous regularity ever since I can remember, namely, to stand up over me, close to me, breathing heavily and smelling of putrid perspiration.

'What, again?' I said to him. 'Not another corny King Kong performance!'

His fist whisked past my snout in playful panto.

'Do grow *up*, Vernon,' I said to him, very patiently. 'You're a big boy now, more than a quarter of a century old.'

What would happen next would be either that he'd push me around in which case, of course, it would be just a massacre, except that he knew I'd get in at least one blow that would really cripple him, and perhaps even harm him for life – or else he'd suddenly feel the whole thing was beneath his dignity, and want to talk to me, talk to anyone, in fact, whatever, since the poor old ape was such an H-Certificate product he was really very lonely.

So he plucked at my short-arse Italian jacket with his great big cucumber fingers and said, 'What you wear this thing for?'

'Excuse me, Vernon,' I said, edging past him to unload my camera on my table. 'I wear it,' I said, taking the jacket off and hanging it up, 'to keep

yobbo (slang) a rude or badly behaved young man **on account of** G. wegen **Julie** girl's name **oafo** oaf; a stupid young man **act** (coll) *here:* G. 'Nummer' **perspiration** sweat **corny** old-fashioned and too well-known **performance** see: act **snout** (slang) nose **panto** pantomime **to grow up** behave like an adult **massacre** ['mæsəkə] **blow** G. Hieb **ape** large monkey **H-certificate** certificate which used to be given to a film stating it was too horrific for children to see **to pluck** pull **short-arse** (slang) very short (of a jacket) **cucumber** G. Gurke **to edge past** move past with small sideways movements warm in winter, and, in summer, to captivate the chicks by swinging my tail around.'

'Hunh!' he said, his mind racing fast, but nothing coming out except this noise like a polar bear with wind. He looked me up and down while his thoughts came into focus. 'Those clothes you wear,' he said at last, 'disgust me.'

And I hope they did! I had on precisely my full teenage drag that would enrage him – the grey pointed alligator casuals, the pink neon pair of ankle crêpe nylon-stretch, my Cambridge blue glove-fit jeans, a vertical-striped happy shirt revealing my lucky neck-charm on its chain, and the Roman-cut short-arse jacket just referred to ... not to mention my wrist identity jewel, and my Spartan warrior hair-do, which everyone thinks costs me 17/6d. in Gerrard Street, Soho, but which I, as a matter of fact, do myself with a pair of nail-scissors and a three-sided mirror that Suzette's got, when I visit her flatlet up in Bayswater, W.2.

'And you, I suppose,' I said, deciding that attack was the best method of defence though oh! so wearisome, 'you imagine you look alluring in that horrible men's wear suiting that you've bought in a marked-down summer sale at the local casbah.'

'It's manly,' he said, 'and it's respectable.'

I gazed at the floppy dung-coloured garments he had on. 'Ha!' was about all I said.

'What's more,' he went on, 'I've not wasted money on it. It's my demobilization suit.'

My heaven, yes, it looked it – *yes*!

'When *you've* done your military service,' the poor old yokel said, his boot face breaking into a crafty grin, 'you'll be given one too, you'll find. *And* a decent hair-cut just for once.'

I gazed at the goon. 'Vernon,' I said, 'I'm sorry for you. Somehow you missed the teenage rave, and you never seem to have had a youth. To try to

to captivate attract and excite **chicks** (slang) girls (outdated American slang) **tail** *here:* G. Hintern **to race** *here:* work **wind** G. Blähung **to come into focus** become clear **to enrage** make very angry **casuals** ['kæʒuəl] shoes without laces **crêpe** [kreɪp] G. Krepp **Cambridge blue** light blue **to reveal** show **charm** G. Anhänger **Roman-cut** Italian-style (short and with narrow lapels) **Spartan** from Sparta in Ancient Greece **warrior** ['wɒrɪə] soldier **hair-do** hair-style **17/6** pre-decimal money: seventeen shillings and sixpence **flatlet** small flat **wearisome** tiring **alluring** attractive **suiting** cloth used to make suits **marked-down** reduced in price **casbah** ['kæzba:] *here:* oriental market **respectable** socially acceptable **floppy** loose **demobilization suit** suit given to soldiers when they were sent home at the end of the war **yokel** simple or stupid country person **crafty** cunning **decent** socially acceptable **goon** stupid person **rave** (coll.) wild party tell you the simplest facts of life is just a waste of valuable breath, however, do try to dig this, if your microbe mini-brain is capable. There's no honour and glory in doing military service, once it's compulsory. If it was voluntary, yes, perhaps, but not if you're just sent.'

'The war,' said Vern, 'was Britain's finest hour.'

'What war? You mean Cyprus, boy? Or Suez? Or Korea?'

'No, stupid. I mean the *real* war, you don't remember.'

'Well, Vernon,' I said, 'please believe me, I'm glad I don't. All of you oldies certainly seem to try to keep it well in mind, because every time I open a newspaper, or pick up a paperback, or go to the Odeon, I hear nothing but war, war, war. You pensioners certainly seem to love that old, old struggle.'

'You're just ignorant,' said Vern.

'Well, if I am, Vern, that's quite okay by me. Because I tell you: not being a mug, exactly, I've no intention of playing soldiers for the simple reasons, first of all, that big armies obviously are no longer necessary, what with the atomic, and secondly, no one is going to tell me to do anything I don't want to, no, or try to blackmail me with that crazy old mixture of threats and congratulations that a pronk like you falls for because you're a born form-filler, tax-payer and cannon-fodder ... well, boy, just take a look in the mirror at yourself.'

That left him silent for a while. 'Come on, now,' I said. 'Be a good half-brother, and let me get on with my work. Why have you moved in this room, anyway?'

'You're wrong!' he cried. 'You'll have to do it!'

'That subject's exhausted. We've been into it thoroughly. Do forget it.'

'What we done, you gotta do.'

'Vernon,' I said, 'I hate to tell you this, but you really don't speak very good English.'

breath [breθ] G. Atem **to dig** (slang) understand (outdated American slang) **compulsory** which must be done by law **Cyprus** ['saɪprəs] island in the Mediterranean; former British colony which gained its independence after a guerilla war fought from 1955–1959 **Suez** ['sʊɪz] canal connecting the Mediterranean with the Red Sea; after Egypt nationalised the canal in 1956 British and French troops invaded the canal zone causing the Suez crisis **Korea** [kə'rɪə] the Korean War, fought from 1950–1953 between North and South Korea; troops from the United States, Britain, and other countries fought on the side of South Korea **to keep s.th. well in mind** remember **paperback** book with a soft paper cover **Odeon** ['əʊdjən] name of a cinema **that's okay by me** (coll.) I've got nothing against that **mug** (coll.) a stupid person who is easily deceived **pronk** (slang) a stupid person **half-brother** only related through one parent **subject** topic **we done** (substandard) we did **you gotta** (coll.) you've got to

'You'll see!'

'All right,' I said, 'I'll see.'

I was trying, as you'll have realized, to drive him out of the room, but the boy is sensitive as the end of a truck, and just flopped back on his bed again, worn out by the mental effort of our conversation. So I put him out of my mind and worked on at my snaps in silence, till Dad knocked on the door with two cups of char; and standing there in the dark, with only the red light burning, we both ignored that moron, not bothering to wonder if he was awake and eavesdropping, or dreaming of winning six Victoria Crosses.

Colin MacInnes (1980), *Absolute Beginners*. London: Alison and Busby. pp. 31–33. The novel was first published in 1959.

sensitive having feelings which are easily hurt **truck** G. Lkw **to flop** fall in a loose and heavy way **worn out** tired, exhausted **to put s.o. out of one's mind** forget s.o. **snap** photo **char** [tʃɑː] (slang) tea **moron** very stupid person **to bother** G. sich die Mühe machen **to wonder** G. sich fragen **to eavesdrop** ['iːvzdrɒp] listen secretly **Victoria Cross** VC; a special medal given to members of the British armed forces for bravery

Comprehension

What evidence is there in the passage for the following statements. If there is no evidence explain what the passage really says.

1. Vernon's bed has no sheets on it because he hasn't got enough money to buy any.
2. It there was a fight between the narrator and Vernon, the narrator thinks he (the narrator) would win.
3. Vernon hasn't got any friends because he looks so ugly.
4. The narrator's hair is very long.
5. Vernon doesn't like his half-brother's clothes because he considers them effeminate.
6. When the narrator asks Vernon, "What war?" it shows that he doesn't know much about recent history.

Topic work

1. Write a brief character study of the narrator, discussing his views, his relationship with his brother and the methods the author uses to characterise him. Discuss and compare your characterisation with those of your fellow students.
2. *Absolute Beginners* was published in 1959. Compare the attitudes and behaviour of the narrator in this novel with those of young people now.

7. Speaker's Corner

And so to the park's edge, overlooking Marble Arch and the old site of Tyburn gallows. When the gallows moved, the hangman's noose was sold. For the old rope, hawkers wanted a shilling an inch. Now gaudy paintings and cheap leather bags litter the railings running west along the Bayswater Road.

But here, men stand on upturned plastic milkcrates and freely bellow things that one day might have hanged them. 'One of the minor wonders of the world,' said Orwell of Speaker's Corner.

On a stepladder over a British Airways bag packed with gospels, a man with a grey moustache, a pea-green shirt, and a look of the lost speaks to a dozen tourists. On the railings behind hangs a notice board. 'Britain Under Judgement', it reads. 'Legalised Abortion' (in red), 'Sodomy' (green), 'No Cure For AIDS Virus'. On the ladder, under his gloved fingers, another notice proclaims the second advent of Christ. It has been proclaiming this every Sunday since 1947.

'When I was in my sins nearly forty years ago,' the man with the moustache shouts urgently, 'I looked alright walking about, but I was a sinner.' Each year, he reckons he introduces 350 people to the gospels in his bag.

to overlook give a view of from above **Marble Arch** situated in the corner of Hyde Park at the junction of Oxford Street and Park Lane; it was designed by John Nash in 1827 and was originally placed outside Buckingham Palace but was moved to its present position in 1851 because it was supposedly too narrow for the royal coach **site** place **Tyburn** Tyburn gallows was London's main place of public execution from the 14th century until 1783; the name is taken from the River Tyburn **gallows** wooden frame from which people are killed by hanging from a rope **noose** [nu:s] ring formed by the end of a rope **hawker** s.o. who sells goods in the street or from door to door **gaudy** ['gɔ:dɪ] with colours which are too bright **to litter** cover in an untidy way **railing** long bars which form a fence **Bayswater Road** road which runs along the north side of Hyde Park **upturned** the bottom is at the top **milkcrate** box made of plastic for carrying milk bottles **to bellow** shout in a deep voice **minor** small, not very important **wonder** ['wʌndə] miracle **George Orwell** pen name of Eric Arthur Blair (1903–1950); English novelist, essayist and journalist; best known for his novels '1984' and 'Animal Farm' **gospel** *here:* bible **moustache** [mə'stɑ:ʃ] hair growing on the upper lip **abortion** G. Abtreibung **AIDS** Acquired Immune Deficiency Syndrome **gloved** [glʌvd] wearing gloves **advent** coming **to reckon** think

Ten yards away, a small man in a brown tweed jacket, from which fluffs a red handkerchief, holds a Bible which has lost its covers. He struts more raucously, in a circle.

'I'm an ex-rapist, robber, thief, alcoholic,' he recites, his eyes focusing on the gaps between his audience. 'Praise the Lord, I'm not drinking. If you're a rapist, if you're a homosexual, you can change your ways. You hear that, lesbians and homosexuals?' he snarls at the much larger gathering next to him, who are listening to a young gay. One or two at the fringe boo him, and he pouts, unsmiling. 'I find a lot of fools in Hyde Park. They think they know all the answers. You may look nice outside, but each single person, each one of you stinks.'

A bearded drunk in a blue wool cap enters the circle, comes up to the speaker, and offers him cider from a yellow plastic bag. The gesture seems more a bribe that a test. 'Talk about yourself a bit more,' urges the drunk.

The man looks through him. 'Are your lives so empty, so lonely and messed up, on a Sunday when it's cold, that all you can do is come here and laugh? I used to come here and laugh. I spent years listening to this. But Jesus can take hold of your life. He can take it and change it. I no longer rob, rape, drink. I work in the poshest club in London . . .'

'Where is it?' asks a black man in a pin-striped suit, suddenly interested.

'If Jesus can change me he can change anybody,' the speaker continues imperviously.

The questioner is not satisfied. 'If you can't tell us where you work, how can we believe you about Jesus?'

Even the policeman, watching, smiles at this. Alert for anything anti-Semitic or treasonable, he monitors from a discreet distance outside the circle. Too close, and the speakers draw him in. It is an offence to break up a meeting, and to hold a meeting within a meeting, which means that a twenty-yard gap is imposed between Americans and communists, Bible-bashers and homosexuals. You never find hecklers speaking, the policeman

yard 0,9144 m **to fluff out of** *here:* G. hervorquellen aus **to strut** G. stolzieren **raucously** ['rɔ:kəslɪ] G. ausgelassen **ex-** former **rapist** a person who has sex with s.o. against his or her will **to focus** concentrate **gap** space **ways** habits; way of life **to snarl** *here:* speak in an angry way **gay** homosexual person **fringe** edge **to boo** show you don't agree by saying 'boo' **to pout** [paʊt] push the lips forward to show displeasure **cider** an alcoholic drink made from apples **gesture** ['dʒestʃə] *here:* an action which is done to show your feelings **bribe** s.th. offered to s.o. in order to get a favour **messed up** ruined **posh** fashionable and expensive **pin-striped** a dark suit with a pattern of thin white lines **imperviously** [ɪm'pɜ:vjəslɪ] *here:* not listening **alert** watchful **treasonable** G. verräterisch **to monitor** *here:* listen very carefully **discreet** tactful **offence** act which is against the law **to impose** force s.o. to accept **Bible-basher** (coll.) s.o. who tries to convert people to Christianity **heckler** s.o. who interrupts a speaker says. He thinks it is a pity there's so much potential which isn't used. The subjects are much the same, and a lot of his time is spent referring speakers to Bow Street when their swearing gets out of hand. At this moment, he has his eyes on that chap over there, an elderly man in a tightly wrapping dark coat. He commands the biggest crowd of all.

'I do not come to educate,' this man shouts, punching his hands and delivering his practised prejudices. 'I come here to upset as many people as I can, and I believe I'm doing quite a good job.' The crowd laughs, appreciatively. 'As a Londoner, I have never done one day's work in my entire life. You people have got to ask yourself one question and one question only. Is it intelligent to work? Now, any comeback on what I've said so far?'

'Who's your shrink?' an American asks quietly, unheard, at the back.

Nicholas Shakespeare (1986), *Londoners.* London: © Sidgwick and Jackson. pp. 222–3.

potential possibility for developing s.th. **to refer s.o. to** *here:* mention s.th. to s.o. **Bow Street** Bow Street Police Court **out of hand** out of control **to command** *here:* attract **prejudice** an opinion formed without deep thought or knowledge **to upset** *here:* make angry **appreciatively** [ə'pri:ʃjətɪvlɪ] showing admiration and pleasure **comeback** answer, reply **shrink** (slang) psychiatrist

Comprehension

1. What does the writer mean when he says that the men at Speaker's Corner are saying things that once 'might have hanged them'?
2. What did George Orwell mean when he wrote that Speaker's Corner was 'one of the minor miracles of the world'?
3. Explain what the man with the moustache means when he says 'I looked alright walking about, but I was a sinner.'
4. Why do you think the gesture of the drunk in offering the cider to the speaker seems 'more a bribe than a test'?
5. Why do you think the black man in the pin-striped suit is described as being 'suddenly interested'?
6. Explain why the policeman smiles when the questioner says, 'If you can't tell us where you work, how can we believe you about Jesus?'
7. Why is it, do you think, that you never find hecklers speaking?
8. What is the effect of referring speakers to Bow Street?
9. What is the writer suggesting when he describes what the man says as 'practised prejudices'.
10. What is the American suggesting when he asks, 'Who's your shrink?'.

Language skills

AIDS is an acronym – a word formed from the initial letters of a group of words. Find out the origin, meaning and pronunciation of the following examples of acronyms:

a) in which the letters are pronounced as a word
1. UNESCO, *2.* NATO, *3.* SCUBA, *4.* RADAR, *5.* LASER, *6.* BASIC, *7.* CAD/CAM, *8.* YUPPIE, *9.* NASA, *10.* WASP

b) which are pronounced as sequences of letters
1. BBC, *2.* EEC, *3.* FBI, *4.* IQ, *5.* A.D., *6.* B.C., *7.* GMT, *8.* AA, *9.* SNP, *10.* pto, *11.* NHS.

Topic work

1. What means, with respect to looks and characteristics, does the writer use to characterise the speakers and what is their effect on the reader?
2. Write a short speech which attempts to bring your fellow students round to your point of view on a controversial topic.

1

2

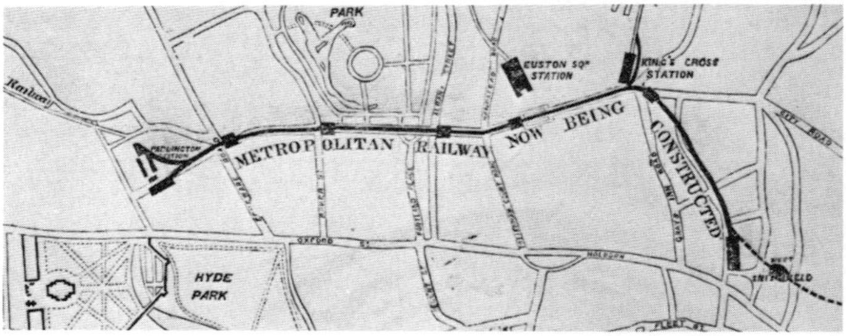

3

(1, 2, 3: *Cassell Ltd.*, London)

GETTING AROUND LONDON

1. The First Underground

Traffic congestion on roads leading into the City was relieved in the south by the river boats. But another solution was needed for the north side of London. It came in the revolutionary idea of an underground railway put forward in the 1830s by a City solicitor, Charles Pearson. He was concerned not so much with traffic as with the difficulties faced by people who were forced to move out of central London when their homes were converted into business premises. Pearson argued that by building an underground railway between the City and Paddington, these people could travel in and out of London daily for a nominal fare. His proposal included a specially planned estate of 10,000 cottages seven miles out.

The estate was never built, but thirty years later he saw his scheme materialize as the Metropolitan Railway. Just under four miles long, it linked Paddington, Euston, and King's Cross stations with the City Terminus near Smithfield. It was the world's first underground railway.

To prevent costly demolition, the line followed the New Road, and at King's Cross turned south-east along and under Farringdon Road. For

congestion very full or blocked because of traffic **to relieve** lessen, reduce **City** an area in central London; the business and financial centre **solicitor** [sə'lɪsɪtə] G. Rechtsanwalt (der nicht vor Gericht plädiert) **premises** a building and the surrounding land **Paddington** a district to the west of central London **nominal** very small **proposal** plan **estate** an area of houses of similar type **scheme** [ski:m] plan **to materialize** become real **to link** join, connect **costly** costing a lot of money **demolition** [demə'lɪʃən] knocking down, destruction of a building once, Parliament raised no objections, and New Road residents agreed, influenced by the plausible argument that it would reduce surface traffic past their doors. Costs were further kept down by 'cut and cover' construction. Instead of tunnelling (as for the Tube later), a trench between 25 and 59 feet deep was cut, the sides revetted with bricks, arched over, and the road replaced.

Work, which started in 1860, took three years. West of King's Cross, the work was easier as the tunnel ran through gravel, and there was only one main sewer, the Tyburn, to be negotiated. But to the east, it ran through clay, and the Fleet Sewer had to be crossed three times. During building the sewer burst, and serious flooding delayed completion. But all was ready for the opening in January 1862.

From the start, the Metropolitan was an immediate success. In the first six months 26,500 people used it daily. With a threepenny fare for the 18-minute Paddington-City journey, the horse bus was outrivalled. And there were cheap fares for workmen, too. The visionary Pearson died three months before the opening.

The way was now open for the whole complex network of lines – the District, Inner Circle, City and South London, and Central – which was to burrow under London in the next fifty years.

Felix Barker and Peter Jackson (1983), *London: 2000 Years of a City and its People.* London: Papermac. p. 306.

for once on this one occasion **resident** person who lives in a house, street or place **plausible** ['plɔ:zɪbəl] seeming to be true or reasonable **Tube** informal name given to the London Underground **trench** long narrow hole cut in the ground **to revet** [rɪ'vet] G. verkleiden **to arch over** [ɑ:tʃ] G. überdachen **gravel** ['grævəl] small stones **sewer** ['su:ə] G. Abwasserrohr **to negotiate** G. überwinden **Fleet** name of a river which is now an underground sewer **completion** [kəm'pli:ʃən] finishing **threepenny** ['θrepnɪ] **to outrival** beat in a competition **visionary** ['vɪʒənrɪ] having the ability to see what the future will be like **to burrow** ['bʌrəʊ] dig

Illustrations on p. 92:

1. Work in progress on the Metropolitan Railway – view from Pentonville Road looking west towards King's Cross.
2. Plan for the Metropolitan Railway, 1860.
3. After this trial trip – immediate success.

Comprehension

Decide what evidence there is in the passage for the following statements:

1. It was easier to get to the City from the south of London than the north.
2. Charles Pearson's aim was to enable people living north of the Thames to get to the City as easily as possible.
3. The housing estate proposed by Charles Pearson was not built because it was situated too far out of London.
4. The route chosen for the underground railway meant that not many houses needed to be knocked down.
5. Before this line was built Parliament had often stopped the building of railway lines in London.
6. Many of the people who used to travel to the City by road would now use the underground railway.
7. The underground railway was more successful than the horse bus because people could get to work more quickly.

Language skills

1. Find examples of the passive voice in this text. Look up the uses of the passive in a grammar and explain why the passive is used in the examples you have found.
2. Write a short summary of the passage giving, as precisely as you can, a chronological sequence to the events described.

Topic work

Imagine you are a reporter interviewing a group of Londoners on the day the underground was opened. Write the questions you would ask and the answers you might have received.

2. Tube Train Driver

Bob has been a motorman – a driver – on the Central line for twenty-two years. Four times a day, for sixty-two hours and £157 a week, he drives from Epping or Hainault to West Ruislip. In twenty-two years he has crossed London roughly 24,000 times.

It is 3.25 p. m. and he is about to start his afternoon shift from Hainault. His morning shift had begun at 6.43 a. m. and taken three hours. 'We never do more than four at a time,' he explains, stepping into the driver's compartment. He carries a black nylon bag containing a tin teapot and two spanners. One spanner he uses to turn a bolt, releasing air pressure; the other, with which he will drive the train, he attaches to the dashboard. His hand must be on this at all times. It is ghoulishly called the 'dead-man's handle'. Should he fall down dead, the train will stop automatically.

The first people to take the 6.43 a. m. from Epping are the postmen, office cleaners and milkmen. There is a short break before the workmen's traffic – painters, plumbers, electricians – and then at 8 a. m. the schoolchildren and office clerks get on.

'You don't get yer gentry till nine. The "nine o'clockers" we used to call them, in their bowler hats. The stationmaster would wait by the barrier, salute them and open the first-class carriage.' Today, the nine o'clockers are the ones who look slowly and grim-faced at their watches. Some embarking at Theydon Bois expect to sit in the same seat every morning.

The last group are 'the womblies', the old-age pensioners who start queuing at 9 a. m. for the cheap rate which begins half an hour later.

Travelling the complete route – the fifty-one miles from Epping to West Ruislip – takes ninety minutes, half of it underground. 'It's easy to get going and think, where am I?' admits Bob. In his mind, London does not begin until he enters the tunnel at Mile End. He is reminded where he is by

the Central line the Underground line that runs from west to east through London **Epping** last station on the eastern end of the Central line **Hainault** ['heɪnɔ:lt] station on the eastern end of the Central line **West Ruislip** ['raɪslɪp] last station on the western end of the Central line **bolt** G. Bolzen **dashboard** the instrument board of a car or train **ghoulishly** ['gu:lɪʃlɪ] G. makaber **plumber** ['plʌmə] person who fits and repairs water pipes and bathroom fittings **yer** [jɜ:] your (imitation of London accent) **gentry** ['dʒentrɪ] people of high social class **Theydon Bois** [ˌθeɪdn'bɔɪz] station on the eastern end of the Central line **Mile End** station on the Central line in the east of London the smell of urine dampening the pillar beside his window. There is a similar pillar and smell at Shepherd's Bush.

The train empties as we make our afternoon journey westwards. In the morning, half get out at Liverpool Street; a replacement quarter – British Rail commuters – get on for Bank, where they are raucously urged by a tape recording to 'Mind the gap'. At Holborn, solicitors step off; at Chancery Lane, postmen and journalists. By the time the early train has reached Bond Street, it is more or less empty. Now, at Oxford Street, American tourists clamber aboard with their day's shopping, making for hotels in Lancaster Gate.

At Queensway, Bob says, people used to come down for the air. The purifying system made it like going to the seaside. No such system exists at Notting Hill Gate, where there is a distinct smell of cooking. Or, more necessarily, at Shepherd's Bush. At Shepherd's Bush the train is delayed. 'The Dosser gang worked here', someone has scrawled on the tunnel wall.

The delay gives one a chance to look back, past the damp pillar, at the station now smartened up with coloured tiles and murals. One or two passengers drift down the platform to the escalators. The down escalator does not work. A man called Bumper Harris was hired to travel up and down the first Underground escalator when it opened at Earl's Court in 1911. He had a wooden leg, and his perambulations were meant to boost the confidence of terrified passengers. Broken-down escalators aside, you cannot imagine London Transport hiring Bumper Harris today. Nor of anyone, like the friend of the writer Ford Madox Ford, who, when dying a long way from London, sighed queerly:

urine ['jʊərɪn] **pillar** G. Säule **Shepherd's Bush** station on the Central line and a district in west London **Liverpool Street** a station on the Central line and also a station for normal trains **replacement** which takes the place of **British Rail** the nationalised company which run Britain's railways **commuter** s.o. who travels a long distance between home and work **Bank** station in the City near the Bank of England **raucously** ['rɔ:kəslɪ] (of voices) in a rough and unpleasant way **to urge** [ɜ:dʒ] try very hard to get s.o. to do s.th. **to mind** be careful of **gap** *here:* space between the train and the platform **Holborn** ['həʊbən] station near to the law courts and law schools **solicitor** [sə'lɪsɪtə] G. Rechtsanwalt (der nicht vor Gericht plädiert) **Chancery Lane** street near Fleet Street and one of London's main post offices **Bond Street** street off Oxford Street, famous for its expensive shops **to clamber** ['klæmbə] **Lancaster Gate** underground station named after a street and a gate to Hyde Park **Queensway** also the name of a street **purifying** making pure, clean **to delay** cause to be late **smartened up** made to look tidier and more elegant **tile** G. Kachel **mural** wall painting **escalator** moving stairs **perambulation** walking about **terrified** very frightened **Ford Madox Ford** (1873–1939), an English writer of German descent for a sight of the gush of smoke that, on the platform of the Underground, one may see escaping in great woolly clots ... He wanted to see it again as others have wished to see once more the Bay of Naples, the olive groves of Catania.

Bob blows his nose. 'When I started,' he says, 'and I blew my nose it would come out black.' He talks about the smog. As a child he would be let off going to school if he could not see the railings opposite. There's still black on station walls, though. People say it's dead skin.

Eventually we continue. Lights twinkle from red to green in the dark until daylight comes at White City, showing the thin, shiny rails hanging down from the tunnel's mouth like walrus teeth. At East Acton, heavy-shouldered men get off for Wormwood Scrubs. Prison officers.

Thereafter London seems to dissolve into back gardens, churchyards and allotments. The open air and green always makes Bob think of his home in Newbury Park. He would like to be walking his dog there now. At Northolt, the smell of toffee on the air reminds him he hasn't booked the Greek restaurant in Gants Hill where he has promised to take the wife. She likes the belly dancing.

At Northolt we come to a buffer. Grabbing his teapot and spanners, Bob walks back through the deserted train. Newspapers lie on the seats. In one carriage there is a paperback. People leave the weirdest things behind, he says. Wheelchairs, outboard motors, kitchen sinks. Once a stuffed gorilla was found. Once a box of glass eyes. Once a bag of human bones.

We drive back into London. Travelling under it from White City is like falling down a bottomless well, broken every now and then by bright lights. On the Underground map, the thick red rule of the Central line insists on the myth of a continuous narrative: a narrative of connected villages, strung out through the city from Ruislip to Epping. In fact, the stations, and the pockets of people lining them, give the impression of beleaguered outposts, not linked in any way except by the dizzying tunnel.

gush G. Schwall **clot** mass, lump **grove** G. Hain **Catania** port in Sicily **White City** station and district in west London **walrus** ['wɔ:lrəs] large sea animal with two long teeth **Wormwood Scrubs** a prison **to dissolve** [dɪ'zɒlv] G. sich auflösen **allotment** a small piece of land on which you can grow vegetables and flowers **Newbury Park** district in east London **Northolt** station and district in west London **Gants Hill** district in east London **belly dancing** G. Bauchtanzen **buffer** G. Puffer **weird** [wɪəd] **wheelchair** chair with wheels used by people who cannot walk **outboard motor** a motor that can be fixed to the back of a small boat **stuffed** (the skin of an animal) filled to make it look real **rule** *here:* line **narrative** *here:* connected series of events **pocket** *here:* small groups **to line** *here:* stand along the inside of **beleaguered** [bɪ'li:gəd] surrounded (by an enemy) **outpost** G. Vorposten **dizzying** making you feel confused and off balance

As with the stations of the Underground map, so with each Londoner. Any attempt to link them, like the names on the Central line, must result in this fictional narrative.

From his 24,000 trips through the city, has Bob gained a sense of how Londoners relate to each other, and the areas in which they live and work? He shakes his head. 'Most of the faces are blurred,' he says, his mind still on the belly dancers of Gants Hill. 'They're just bodies.'

Nicholas Shakespeare (1986), *Londoners.* London: © Sidgwick and Jackson. pp. 6–10.

blurred unclear

Comprehension

1. Follow Bob's journey along the Central Line and as far as possible give the following details in note form about each station that he stops at:
   – the time of arrival, if given
   – the people who get on or off the train, giving the reason why they are at this station at this particular time
   – any special features of the station
2. Why do you think the writer says that
   'you cannot imagine London Transport hiring Bumper Harris today' (l. 49–50) or that anyone would sigh queerly
   'for the sight of the gush of smoke that, on the platform of the Underground, one may see escaping in great woolly clots . . .' (l. 53/54)?
3. What does the writer mean when he calls what he has written a
   'fictional narrative'?

Topic work

1. How does the writer manage to turn the description of what is an everyday, comparatively unexciting activity into an amusing and interesting account?
   – Analyse the writer's style.
   – Study the details he chooses to describe.
   – Discuss his use of anecdotes and driver's comments.
2. Write an account of the day in the life of an ordinary job with which you are acquainted. Try to add the kind of interesting details that are included in this passage.

CITIES FOR CARS, OR . . .

...CITIES FOR PEOPLE?

3. Cities for Cars – Cities for People

Cities for Cars

Congestion

The theory is that we need new roads to relieve traffic congestion. In fact, new roads often encourage more traffic, which means *more* congestion! Even widening existing roads can draw large amounts of additional traffic into city centres, many of which are ill-equipped to deal with the problem. And it's often the car commuters that cause so much of the problem. One person's car can easily become another person's traffic jam!

Accidents

More than 5,000 people are killed every year on Britain's roads, at a cost to the country of £ 2.7 billion, according to Department of Transport figures. In London alone, 566 people were killed and 50,000 injured during 1984.

Disruption

New roads schemes, or even the threat of them, can cast a terrible planning blight over large parts of local communities. Whole areas can rapidly become very tatty, property values fall, businesses move out and the vandals move in. When the roads do come, as happened with the Westway, they can literally rip the community apart, slicing throught residential areas, cutting off homes from shops, schools, hospitals and places where people work. As always, it tends to be the old, the disabled, the young, and women who suffer the most.

congestion when roads are very full or blocked **to relieve** [rɪ'li:v] lessen **additional** more **ill-equipped** not having what is necessary **commuter** s.o. who regularly travels a long distance between home and work **billion** one thousand million **scheme** [ski:m] plan **to cast a blight over** make things seem ugly, unpleasant **tatty** (coll.) untidy, in a bad condition **property** *here:* buildings **vandal** ['vændəl] s.o. who enjoys damaging and destroying things **Westway** G. Stadtautobahn durch West-London **literally** really **to rip apart** tear into two parts **to slice** cut **to tend to** G. dazu neigen

Emissions
Car exhaust fumes are unpleasant, dirty and dangerous. They are a threat to human health, even involving certain cancer forming agents, and a threat to the environment throught the acid rain they help to cause. And *lead* still won't be taken out of petrol until the EEC directive is complied with in 1989.

Employment
As far as the local community is concerned, new roads usually destroy more jobs than they create. Houses and factories may be knocked down, never to be rebuilt; firms can locate outside the area and drive their products into the city from there. As if the lorries weren't already enough of a problem, as they thunder through our cities, polluting the atmosphere, deafening us, and causing untold damage to our homes and roads.

Cities for People

Public Transport
A proper balance between cars an cities *is* possible. This applies just as much to local residents with cars and to drivers of essential vehicles, as to those who do *not* drive. With the right kind of planning and investment, public transport *works*. Train, bus, tube, metro, tram – these are the most reliable ways of moving large numbers of people efficiently. Local authorities such as Sheffield, Newcastle and (when they were allowed to!) the GLC, have shown just what can be done to provide clean, fast and frequent public services.

exhaust fumes gases emitted by cars **threat** [θret] G. Drohung **cancer** G. Krebs **agent** substance **environment** the natural world around us **lead** [led] soft heavy metal added to petrol **EEC** European Economic Community **directive** official order or instruction **to comply with** follow (an order) **to locate** G. sich niederlassen **to pollute** make dirty **untold** too much to be counted **resident** s.o. who lives in a place **investment** putting money into a project **tube** name given to the London Underground **metro** underground railway system **local authority** government of a particular area or city **GLC** Greater London Council; the body which governed London until its abolition in 1986

Lorries

Many countries now ban most lorries in their towns at weekends and on public holidays. Our local authorities have the power to ban heavy lorries too, and the GLC has just introduced a night-time and weekend lorry ban. And much more of our freight could be moved by rail

Road Safety

Road safety and better streets go hand in hand. Local authorities can create "play streets" or "environmental areas" where through-traffic is kept out with road closures and one-way systems, without seriously inconveniencing local traffic. Both cycling and walking are healthy, cheap and much better for the environment than over-dependence on the motor car. But they need to be positively encouraged, as they are in Europe.

Jobs

Many authorities are now putting more emphasis on setting up local employment initiatives, but we could still be doing far more in terms of repairing and renovating our housings, tidying up derelict land, planting more trees, or providing more allotments for people to grow food. "Greening the city" means we should *all* benefit!

Communities

Communities are held together by invisible threads, by neighbours helping each other out, by being able to recognise people in the street rather than everyone being strangers, with kids being able to walk to school, and people using the shop on the corner rather than driving miles to the nearest hyper-market. That's what many people believe *quality of life* is really about.

heavy lorry large vehicle for carrying goods **environmental area** specially protected area **closure** ['kləʊʒə] **to put emphasis on** G. etwas betonen **local employment initiative** special action in an area to help people without work to find jobs **in terms of** in the form of **to tidy up** put in order **derelict** old and falling into ruin **allotment** *here:* G. Schrebergarten **to benefit** be useful, helpful to **kid** (coll.) child

Comprehension

Summarise as briefly as possible the arguments made in 'Cities for Cars' against the use of cars in cities and those given in 'Cities for People' for the changes proposed by Friends of the Earth. Use the headings given in the advertisement and sum up each section in just one sentence.

Topic work

1. Discuss the aims and effectiveness of the leaflet 'Cities for Cars – Cities for People' under the following headings:
   - What is the function of this leaflet?
   - How effective is the leaflet in getting across its message?
   - Has this been got across to the reader effectively?
   - Discuss the arguments given in 'Cities for Cars' and 'Cities for People' which you summarised in the comprehension section. How convincing are they?
   - Can you think of better arguments and counter-arguments?
   - Is the advertisement mainly persuasive or is it also informative? Explain why.
2. After reading the next text IV.4 Move to 'bury' London's traffic crisis, organise a debate on the motion: The proposal to build a system of road tunnels under London is the only way to solve London's traffic problems and should be implemented immediately.
3. Friends of the Earth is a pressure group dedicated to reducing environmental pollution. Think about pollution in the town or area where you live and ways to reduce it. Prepare a report and present it to your class for discussion.

4. Move to 'bury' London's Traffic Crisis

Department of Transport engineers are examining a proposal to divert half the capital's traffic below the surface in a 70-mile network of underground tunnels.

The £5.5 billion plan has been given more urgency after two weeks of the worst pre-Christmas traffic jams the city has seen. It is backed by an anonymous consortium which includes a leading firm of architects and one of the top construction companies.

Its promoters claim it would cure crippling traffic congestion, as well as reduce noise and fumes. The scheme would be financed by private investors and repaid from a £2 toll paid by drivers.

The proposals are among a number submitted by private developers to the Department of Transport for coping with the rapid growth of traffic on Britain's roads.

Transport officials are privately worried that without drastic improvements in London, the traffic crisis will worsen. Already there are more than 1.5 m vehicle move-

The Times, 27 January 1989. (*Times Newspapers Ltd.* 1989)

move *here:* plan **Department of Transport** the government department (formerly called Ministry) responsible for transport **proposal** plan, suggestion **billion** one thousand million **urgency** G. Dringlichkeit **pre-** before **traffic jam** when so many cars are using the roads and can only move slowly **to back** *here:* support financially **consortium** [kən'sɔ:tjəm] **promoter** s.o. who helps actively to form or arrange a project or business **crippling** *here:* so bad it brings s.th. to a stop **congestion** when roads are very full or blocked **scheme** [ski:m] plan **investor** s.o. who puts money into a business project **to submit** G. unterbreiten **to cope with** deal successfully with a difficult situation ments in the capital each day – a total which is expected to increase.

The scheme, described as no more costly or ambitious than the Channel tunnel, would consist of six 80 ft-deep "underways", three running north to south and three east to west. Each would link up with a national motorway. At "interchange points", where the motorways cross British Rail or London Underground lines, underground parking would be provided to allow drivers to continue their journey by train.

Jerry Matthews, chairman of Covell Matthews International, one of the backers, claims that tunnels are the only answer to traffic congestion. "None of the proposals put forward in the last five years is capable of easing London's traffic problems," he said. "Flyovers and road improvement schemes only provide temporary stop-gaps. This scheme is viable; it can pay its own keep and needs only the government's sanction."

The proposals have been welcomed by road and environment lobbies, including the British Road Federation and the Noise Abatement Society, which want urgent action on traffic congestion, public transport hold-ups, pollution, road safety, parking and "rat running" – taking shortcuts.

A typical London driver spends 111 hours a year sitting in stationary or slow traffic. The total cost in wasted time and fuel is estimated at £1.4 billion, an annual bill of £500 each. The roads have become so clogged that in the heart of the city vehicles travel at only 8mph – as slowly as a horse and cart did 100 years ago.

Some experts are sceptical about the scheme and believe it would encourage more drivers into the capital. Martin Mogridge, of University College's transport studies group, said: "Building more roads will mean more cars and more congestion".

ambitious [æm'bɪʃəs] G. kühn **chairman** s.o. who directs the meetings of the directors of a company **to claim** *here:* state that s.th. is true **to put forward** suggest **flyover** a place where two roads cross each other at different levels **temporary** lasting only for a limited period of time **stop-gap** s.th. which fills a need for a time until a better one is found **viable** ['vaɪəbl] **to pay its keep** G. ein rentables Geschäft sein **sanction** official acceptance, approval **environment** the world around us **British Road Federation** a pressure group with the aim of persuading the government to build more roads **Noise Abatement Society** a pressure group with the aim of persuading the government to reduce noise pollution **hold-up** delay **pollution** making dirty **rat running** (coll.) taking a shorter or quicker route **vehicle** ['vi:ɪkl] G. Fahrzeug **sceptical** ['skeptɪkl] **University College** a separate part, a college, of the University of London

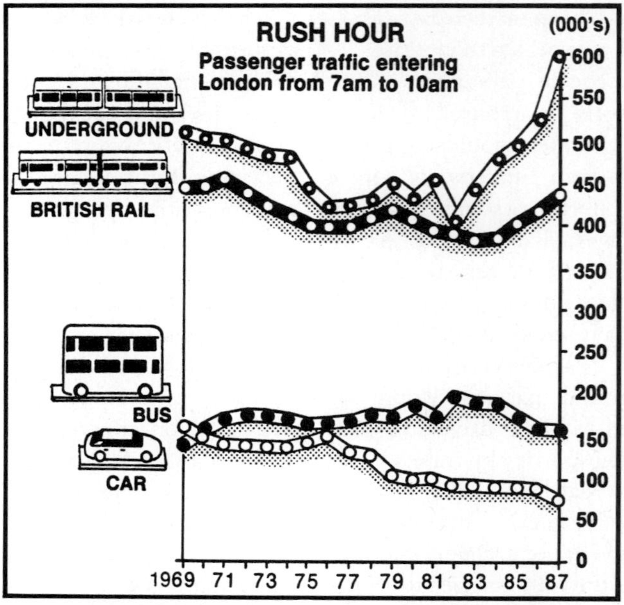

The Times 6 December 1988. (*Times Newspapers Ltd.* 1988)

Comprehension

Give brief answers to the following questions, without, if possible, looking at the passage again.

1. Whose proposal is it to build the road tunnels under London?
2. What event made people realise the urgency of London's road traffic problems?
3. What are the advantages of the proposed road tunnels?
4. Describe the scheme briefly.
5. Why is such a radical scheme necessary?
6. Why do some experts doubt that the scheme will solve London's traffic problems?

Language skills

1. Match the following definitions to words in the text:
   (Paragraphs 1, 2 and 3)
   a) make someone change from one direction or route to another;
   b) a group of companies which work together on a project;
   c) gas from motors or machines;
   d) money you pay to use a road, bridge or tunnel;
   (Paragraphs 4, 5 and 6)
   e) someone who hopes to make a profit from building something;
   f) costing a lot of money;

g) place where different means of transport meet;
(Paragraphs 7 and 8)
h) improving; making better;
i) able to succeed;
j) groups of people who try to persuade the government to support their aims;
k) a quicker route;
(Paragraph 9)
l) not moving;
m) blocked;
n) not willing to believe something.

2. Collect as many terms as you can from the text associated with 'traffic'.

Topic work

1. a) Discuss the diagram on p. 108. In particular try to find reasons for the decline and increase in use of the four main means of transport given.
   b) Imagine you are an official at the Department of Transport. Bearing in mind the diagram on p. 108, what you have read in the text *Cities for Cars – Cities for People* and what you have read in the above text, write an objective report on the plan to build the underground road tunnels, concluding with your recommendations.

5. The Class of 7.47

It takes something startling to persuade commuters to break stride as they hurry from their trains towards the platform barrier on the way to work. At Victoria the other morning, a little before 9 am, people stepping from the 7.47 from Brighton stopped and listened, scarcely believing their ears. What they seemed to hear from one of the carriage windows was a familiar strain by Schubert, sung in a foreign tongue:

Dans un ruisseau limpide
La truite allait nageant
Frétillante et rapide
Ainsi qu'un trait d'argent...

commuter s.o. who regularly travels long distances to work **to break stride** *here:* start running **barrier** fence or railings at a station where you show your ticket **Victoria** Victoria Station; main London station serving the south of England and the Continent **strain** tune, melody **tongue** *here:* language

Singing? At that unfestive hour? And in French?

They had, though few knew it, been travelling on a 'brain train', one of a growing number where groups of commuters get together at fixed times each week to improve their minds, exploiting time otherwise squandered on the routine journey between home and work.

Ellen Lippa's French class is one of the longest established and the best organised. A vivacious Frenchwoman, and a teacher of long experience, she has for the last eight years been travelling from her Brighton home to London with her class of eight, every Tuesday and Thursday morning. They pay £18 each for an academic term of ten weeks. The course is organised by the Further Education Department at Sussex University in co-operation with the Commuter Study Club, a small agency funded by British Rail to arrange mobile classes in a wide range of subjects.

Mrs Lippa, a small, pert woman in a suit with a white beret and glasses, has to be sure she is at Brighton station by 7.30 am, to be on hand when the empty train draws into

the platform. BR will not let her use a first-class compartment and most standard seats are in open-plan carriages, unsuitable for teaching. But each first-class carriage has a single standard-class compartment at one end, seating eight. She must be sure to stake a claim to one of these and having done so, plasters the windows with stickers announcing 'French class', to warn off others and help the students find her. The pupils arrive in a bunch, five minutes before departure time. Wendy Snook, who has been in the class two years, is a financial analyst

unfestive (hum.) *here:* early; i.e. when you don't feel very happy **to exploit** use for your own advantage **to squander** ['skwɒndə] waste **vivacious** [vɪ'veɪʃəs] lively **term** fixed period of time in the school or university year **Further Education** education for people over the age of 16 **Sussex** county to the south of London **Sussex University** located near Brighton **agency** *here:* business that makes its money by bringing people into contact with other people **to fund** give money **pert** G. kess **on hand** ready when needed **to draw into** *here:* drive into **open-plan** not divided into small compartments **to stake a claim** state that you have a right to s.th. **to plaster** *here:* cover **to warn off** make s.o. go away **financial analyst** s.o. who analyses the financial situation of a company with a US company in East Croydon. Adrian Carrick, an architect who occasionally needs French for work and holidays, is in his second term. Helen Fox, a secretary in the European circulation department of *The Economist*, has a degree in French and German but uses German more often in her work. She found her French was getting rusty.

'I've only just moved to Brighton,' she explains. 'When I started commuting they put a leaflet in the train with a number to ring if we were interested in classes. I'm glad I signed up. I enjoy it and I feel I'm doing something useful with my time.'

Others in the class are Steve Perry, a civil servant at the Department of Trade and Industry; Linda Austin, a training officer for a trade union; and Corrinne Filmer, a computer programmer.

The train pulls out on time: '*Notre conversation commence,*' announces Ellen, framed in the compartment doorway. Officially the class does not start until Haywards Heath, when the last member gets on, but before that they work up some useful chat about their jobs, what they had for dinner, the weather ... Ellen is skilled at establishing a cordial *ambiance* in her mobile schoolroom. A little music works well. 'Sometimes I bring my mandolin and we sing French songs, but it is too heavy to take every time. At Christmas we all get together for an end-of-term drink at a Brighton pub.'

Five minutes out, at Preston Park, the newest recruit joins us. He is Matthew O'Shaughnessy, who works for Eurotunnel: no need to explain why he needs French. At 8.07 am the train arrives at Haywards Heath and the class is completed by the arrival of David Blocker, a banker.

'*Bonjour*, David.' Ellen explains in French what they have done so far. More students give readings and get tips on pronunciation. She

East Croydon suburb of London **occasionally** from time to time, not regularly **circulation** the number of copies of a newspaper or magazine that are sold **The Economist** a weekly magazine dealing with economics and financial matters **degree** title given to a student who has completed a course of study **rusty** (coll.) G. aus der Übung **leaflet** small piece of paper giving information **to ring** (coll.) telephone **civil servant** s.o. who works for the national government **Department of Trade and Industry** government department, headed by a Secretary of State (minister) **training officer** G. Mitarbeiter im Ausbildungsbereich **trade union** G. Gewerkschaft **to pull out** *here:* leave **on time** at the right time **Haywards Heath** town in Sussex **to work up** *here:* practise **chat** informal talk **skilled** able to do s.th. well **cordial** warm, friendly **ambiance** (Fr) ['æmbɪəns] atmosphere **out** away, from the start **Preston Park** suburb of Brighton **recruit** [rɪ'kru:t] **O'Shaughnessy** [əʊ'ʃɔ:nəsɪ] **Eurotunnel** the company set up to organise the building of the Channel Tunnel gives back last week's homework and sets a translation assignment. Then it is time for a dictation.

Wendy leaves at East Croydon but the others stick to it doggedly until Clapham Junction where Ellen, despite the lack of her mandolin, suggests a song. Nervous at first, the class soon warms to it. Obligingly, the train halts for a minute or two just before Victoria: time for an extra verse before they begin their day's work. Ellen is sure this gentle mental exercise pays off later in the office. 'It puts you in the mood for work,' she says.

to set an assignment give s.o. a task **to stick to** not give up **doggedly** ['dɒgɪdlɪ] refusing to give up even when faced with difficulties **Clapham Junction** ['klæpəm] place in south London where many railway lines meet **despite** in spite of **lack of** not having **to warm to s.th.** become more enthusiastic about s.th. **obligingly** helpfully **to halt** [hɔ:lt] stop **to pay off** G. sich auszahlen

Language skills

After checking in a grammar what phrasal verbs are, find eight phrasal verbs in the passage.
Using an English language dictionary find other verbs meaning the same as the phrasal verbs.

Topic work

1. Write a fictional interview with
   - Mrs Ellen Lippa
   - two of the commuters who are learning French with her.

   Compare the interviews with those of other students. Decide which are most realistic and authentic and which are most amusing.
2. Discuss the advantages and disadvantages of long-distance commuting.

6. Sweet Thames Flow Softly – a ballad

Sweet Thames Flow Softly

I met my girl at Woolwich Pier, beneath a big crane standing,
And, Oh, the love I felt for her it passed all understanding.
Took her sailing on the river,
flow, sweet river, flow,
London Town was mine to give her,
sweet Thames flow softly.
Made the Thames into a crown,
flow, sweet river, flow,
Made a brooch of Silvertown,
sweet Thames flow softly.

At London Yard I held her hand, at Blackwall Point I faced her,
At the Isle of Dogs I kissed her mouth and tenderly embraced her.
Heard the bells of Greenwich ringing,
flow, sweet river, flow,
All the time my heart was singing,
sweet Thames flow softly.
Limehouse Reach I gave her there,
flow, sweet river, flow,
As a ribbon for her hair,
sweet Thames flow softly.

Woolwich ['wʊlɪtʃ] district in south-east London, just south of the Thames; part of the London Borough of Greenwich **crane** machine for lifting heavy objects using a long movable arm **brooch** [brəʊtʃ] small decorative object worn on women's clothes, fixed on by a pin **Silvertown** district in east London on the north bank of the Thames opposite Woolwich; part of the London Borough of Barking **London Yard** dockyard on the south bank of the Thames **Blackwall Point** point on the south bank of the Thames near the Blackwall Tunnel **Isle of Dogs** district in London's docklands, surrounded on three sides by the Thames; part of the London Borough of Tower Hamlets **Limehouse Reach** stretch of the river on the west side of the Isle of Dogs

From Shadwell Dock to Nine Elms Reach we cheek to cheek were dancing,
Her necklace, made of London Bridge, her beauty was enhancing.
Kissed her once again at Wapping,
flow, sweet river, flow,
After that there was no stopping,
sweet Thames flow softly.
Richmond Park it was her ring,
flow, sweet river, flow,
I'd have given her anything,
sweet Thames flow softly.

From Rotherhithe to Putney Bridge my love I was declaring,
And she, from Kew to Isleworth, her love to me was swearing.
Love had set my heart a-burning,
flow, sweet river, flow,
Never saw the tide was turning,
sweet Thames flow softly.
Gave her Hampton Court to twist,
flow, sweet river, flow,
Into a bracelet for her wrist,
sweet Thames flow softly.

Now, alas, the tide has changed, my love she has gone from me,
And winter's frost has touched my heart and put a blight upon me.
Creeping fog is on the river,
flow, sweet river, flow,
Sun and moon and stars gone with her,
sweet Thames flow softly.

Shadwell Dock dock on the north bank of the Thames **Nine Elms Reach** stretch of the river between Vauxhall Bridge and Chelsea Bridge **necklace** ['neklıs] decorative chain worn round the neck **to enhance** increase **Wapping** ['wɒpıŋ] district in east London **Richmond Park** royal park in south-west London **Rotherhithe** district in south-east London, on the south bank of the Thames opposite Wapping **Putney Bridge** bridge across the Thames in south-west London **Kew** [kju:] district in west London **Isleworth** ['aızlwəθ] district in west London **Hampton Court** district and palace on the River Thames in south-west London **bracelet** decorative band or ring worn round the wrist **blight** *here:* a feeling of great unhappiness

Swift the Thames runs to the sea,
flow, sweet river, flow,
Bearing ships and part of me,
sweet Thames flow softly.

Ewan MacColl (1979)

Kenneth Baker (ed.) (1984), *London Lines.* London: Methuen. p. 138.

Topic work

1. Summarise what the poem/song is about in a few sentences.
2. Explain the following expressions in your own words:
   (l. 3) '... passed all understanding'
   (l. 37) 'Never saw the tide was turning'
   (l. 51) 'Bearing ships and part of me'
3. a) Explain the significance of the River Thames for the poem.
   b) Explain the significance of the place names for the poem.
   c) Evaluate the imagery and language of the poem; how does the language of the poem compare with a prose rendering of the story?
4. Characterise the relationship between the poet and the woman.

7. A Trip on the River

I have still other memories of Greenwich, where there is a charming old park, on a summit of one of whose grassy undulations the famous observatory is perched. To do the thing completely you must take passage upon one of the little grimy sixpenny steamers that ply upon the Thames, perform the journey by water, and then, disembarking, take a stroll in the park

Greenwich ['grɪnɪdʒ] district in south-east London **charming** very pleasing **summit** top of a hill or mountain **undulation** rising and falling like a wave **observatory** place from which scientists watch the sky **to be perched** *here:* be situated on a high place **to take passage** (arch.) make a journey **grimy** ['graɪmɪ] covered with dirt **steamer** steam-powered boat **to ply** travel regularly **to disembark** [ˌdɪsɪm'bɑ:k] get off (a boat) **to take a stroll** go for a walk slowly to get up an appetite for dinner. I find an irresistible charm in any sort of river-navigation, but I scarce know how to speak of the little voyage from Westminster Bridge to Greenwich. It is in truth the most prosaic possible form of being afloat, and to be recommended rather to the inquiring than to the fastidious mind. It initiates you into the duskiness, the blackness, the crowdedness, the intensely commercial character of London. Few European cities have a finer river than the Thames, but none certainly has expended more ingenuity in producing a sordid river-front. For miles and miles you see nothing but the sooty backs of warehouses, or perhaps they are the sooty faces: in buildings so utterly expressionless it is impossible to distinguish. They stand massed together on the banks of the wide turbid stream, which is fortunately of too opaque a quality to reflect the dismal image. A damp-looking, dirty blackness is the universal tone. The river is almost black, and is covered with black barges; above the black housetops, from among the far-stretching docks and basins, rises a dusky wilderness of masts. The little puffing steamer is dingy and gritty – it belches a sable cloud that keeps you company as you go. In this carboniferous shower your companions, who belong chiefly, indeed, to the classes bereft of lustre, assume an harmonious grayness; and the whole picture, glazed over with the glutinous London mist, becomes a masterly composition. But it is very impressive in spite of its want of lightness and brightness, and though it is ugly it is anything but trivial. Like so many of the aspects of English civilisation that are untouched by elegance or grace, it has the merit of expressing something very serious. Viewed in this intellectual light the polluted river, the sprawling barges, the deadfaced warehouses, the frowsy people, the atmospheric impurities become richly suggestive. It sounds

irresistible which is impossible to resist **navigation** travelling in a boat **scarce** (arch.) hardly **prosaic** dull, uninteresting **afloat** floating on water **fastidious** [fə'stɪdɪəs] difficult to please **to initiate** [ɪ'nɪʃɪeɪt] introduce **duskiness** dark colour **to expend** spend, use **ingenuity** [ˌɪndʒɪ'nu:ətɪ] skill, cleverness **sordid** dirty **sooty** ['sʊti] G. rußig **warehouse** large building for storing things **utterly** completely **turbid** not clear, muddy **stream** (arch.) river **opaque** [əʊ'peɪk] not able to be seen through, not transparent **dismal** sad, gloomy **tone** *here:* colour **barge** [bɑ:dʒ] boat used for carrying goods on a river **dusky** dark-coloured **to puff** blow out smoke or steam **dingy** ['dɪndʒɪ] dirty **gritty** covered with small pieces of dirt **to belch** *here:* throw out in large quantities **sable** black or very dark **carboniferous** [ˌkɑ:bɔ'nɪfərəs] containing coal **bereft of** (arch.) not having, without **lustre** ['lʌstə] bright shining appearance **to assume** begin to have **to glaze over** give a shiny, glass-like surface to **glutinous** ['glu:tɪnəs] sticky **composition** [ˌkɒmpə'zɪʃn] G. Zusammensetzung **impressive** G. imponierend **anything but** G. alles anders als **polluted** dirty **sprawling** spread over a wide area **frowsy** ['fraʊzi] shabby, not neat or clean **impurities** dirty substances **suggestive** giving a certain impression rather absurd, but all this smudgy detail may remind you of nothing less than the wealth and power of the British Empire at large; so that a kind of metaphysical magnificence hovers over the scene, and supplies what may be literally wanting. I don't exactly understand the association, but I know that when I look off to the left at the East India Docks, or pass under the dark hugely piled bridges, where the railway trains and the human processions are for ever moving, I feel a kind of imaginative thrill. The tremendous piers of the bridges, in especial, seem the very pillars of the Empire aforesaid.

Henry James (1981), *English Hours.* Oxford: Oxford University Press. pp. 94–5. The collection of articles was first published in 1905.

smudgy G. verschmiert **to hover** ['hɒvə] stay in the air in one place **literally** G. buchstäblich **to be wanting** *here:* missing **procession** a line of people, vehicles moving along together **thrill** G. Erregung **pier** *here:* G. Pfeiler **in especial** (arch.) especially **pillar** G. Pfeiler **aforesaid** (arch.) talked about before

Comprehension

What does the writer praise and what does he find fault with during his trip on the river?
How does he reconcile the negative and positive aspects of what he experiences?

Language skills

List as many adjectives as you can find in the text connected with 'dirt'.
Using an English language dictionary give a definition of the words which makes the differences in meaning between them clear.
Find out the nouns or verbs from which the adjectives are derived.

Topic work

This simple journey on a steamer inspires the writer to make interesting comments on what he sees: on the places, on the people, and on their culture and history.
Think of an excursion you have made and write a similar account.

TRADE, INDUSTRY, AND COMMERCE

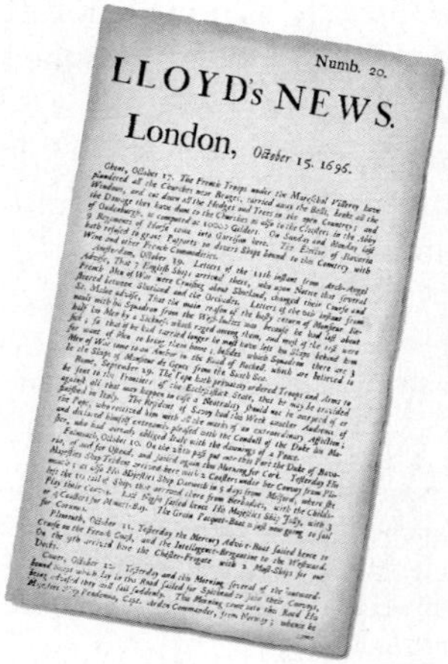
Numb. 20.

LLOYD's NEWS.

London, October 15. 1696.

A Dream
Forget six counties overhung with smoke,
Forget the snorting steam and piston stroke,
Forget the spreading of the hideous town;
Think rather of the pack horse on the down,
And dream of London, small and white and clean,
The clear Thames bordered by gardens green.

William Morris (1834–1896)

1. Lloyd's of London: Edward Lloyd's Coffee House

Today Lloyd's bears little outward resemblance to the noisy, dim and smoke-filled coffee house where it all started 300 years ago. Yet a proper understanding of the present-day Lloyd's, how it works, why it exists even, is impossible without a brief glimpse at the past.

In the 17th century the insurance of ships and cargoes was a fairly simple matter of hawking a policy round the City for subscription by anyone with sufficient means to take a share of the risk in return for a percentage of the premium. The insurance broker was skilled in ensuring that policies were

Lloyd's [lɔɪdz] a leading international insurance market; not an insurance company **to bear** *here:* have, show **resemblance** similarity **cargo** goods carried by ship, plane, train or lorry **to hawk** sell on the street or from door to door **the City** the City of London **subscription** agreement to pay regularly for something **sufficient** [sə'fɪʃənt] enough **means** *here:* money **percentage** [pə'sentɪdʒ] G. Prozentsatz **premium** payment made to buy insurance **broker** *here:* s.o. who sells insurance **skilled** having a special ability **to ensure** [ɪnʃʊə] make sure, certain **policy** a written statement of the details of an agreement with an insurance company

(Fotomax Index)

underwritten only by men of sufficient financial integrity to meet their share of a claim to the full extent, if need be, of their personal fortunes. Underwriters were in the main wealthy merchants, signing policies as a sideline to their main business.

It was against this background that Edward Lloyd opened his coffee house in Tower Street close to the Tower of London some time in 1688. Although remarkably little is known about this enterprising Welshman or his establishment, it seems very likely that, from the outset, he encouraged a clientele of merchants, shipowners, sea captains and others with an interest in waterborne trade. Coffee houses, of which there were many hundreds in London at that time, were centres of discussion, where business

to underwrite write your name under an insurance policy and therefore take responsibility for fulfilling it **integrity** honesty **to meet a claim** pay s.o. money owing from an insurance policy **extent** G. Ausmaß **if need be** if necessary **fortune** money and possessions **sideline** an activity in addition to one's regular job **remarkably** surprisingly **enterprising** being willing to take risks or do s.th. new **Welshman** man from Wales **establishment** *here:* firm, business **outset** beginning **clientele** [ˌkliːən'tel] customers **waterborne** carried on water and pleasure were happily combined and where the latest gossip could be heard. Further, Edward Lloyd gained a reputation for providing trustworthy shipping news. This was one of the most important factors in successful underwriting and perhaps more than anything else ensured that Lloyd's, over and above its rivals, eventually became the recognised place to obtain marine insurance.

As far as is known, Edward Lloyd himself took no part in underwriting. He was described in his day mostly as a 'coffee man' and seemed content to provide his patrons with congenial surroundings and the simple facilities they needed to do business with each other. When Lloyd died in 1713 his principal legacy to the future was his name and the establishment bearing it.

Lloyd's of London, Lime Street London EC3M 7HA.
Pictures reproduced by courtesy of Lloyd's of London.

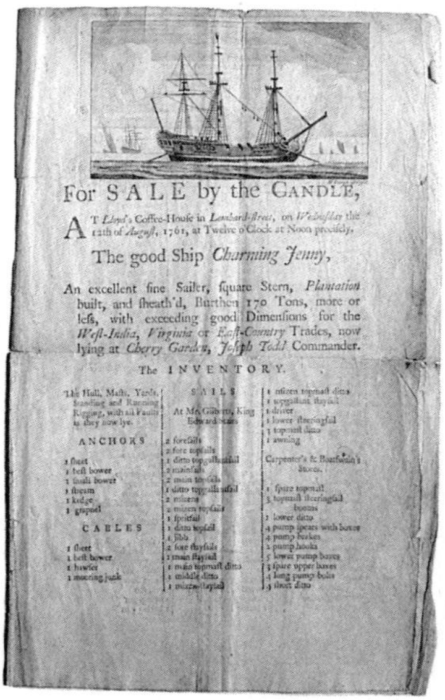

For SALE by the CANDLE,

AT *Lloyd's* Coffee-House in *Lombard-street*, on *Wednesday* the 12th of *August*, 1761, at Twelve o'Clock at Noon precisely.

The good Ship *Charming Jenny*,

An excellent fine Sailer, square Stern, *Plantation* built, and sheath'd, Burthen 170 Tons, more or less, with exceeding good Dimensions for the *West-India*, *Virginia* or *East-Country* Trades, now lying at *Cherry Garden*, *Joseph Todd* Commander.

The INVENTORY.

The Hull, Masts, Yards, Standing and Running Rigging, with all Faults as they now lye.

ANCHORS

1 sheet
1 best bower
1 small bower
1 stream
1 kedge
1 grapnel

CABLES

1 sheet
1 best bower
1 hawser
1 mooring junk

SAILS

At Mr. Gilberts, King Edward stairs

2 foresails
2 fore topsails
1 ditto topgallantsail
2 mainsails
2 main topsails
1 ditto topgallantsail
2 mizens
2 mizen topsails
1 spritsail
1 ditto topsail
2 jibbs
2 fore staysails
1 main staysail
1 main topmast ditto
1 middle ditto
1 mizen staysail
1 mizen topmast ditto
1 topgallant staysail
1 driver
1 lower steeringsail
3 topmast ditto
1 awning

Carpenter's & Boatswain's Stores.

1 spare topmast
3 topmast steeringsail booms
1 lower ditto
4 pump spears with boxes
4 pump brakes
2 pump hooks
5 lower pump boxes
3 spare upper boxes
4 long pump bolts
3 short ditto

gossip conversation about the details of other people's private lives **trustworthy** reliable **underwriting** *here:* being an insurer, taking insurance risks **rival** s.o. with whom you compete **eventually** in the end **marine** connected with ships **patron** ['peɪtrən] *here:* customer **congenial** [kən'dʒi:nɪəl] pleasant **surroundings** *here:* place, everything that surrounds you **facilities** things that are useful **legacy** *here:* s.th. you leave behind for other people **to bear** *here:* carry

Comprehension

1. How would someone in the 17th century have gone about insuring a ship or a cargo?
2. What was the most important thing an insurance broker had to be sure of before he accepted a risk?

3. Why did underwriters have to be very wealthy?
4. Give three reasons why an insurance market should have become established in Edward Lloyd's coffee shop.

Language skills

1. Collect as many terms as you can find in the text connected with 'insurance'. Check their meanings in the annotations.
2. 'Eventually' (l. 347) is a false friend, a word that looks as if it means the same as a similar sounding or looking German word, but in fact means something different. Check the meanings of the following English 'false friends' and compare them with their German 'look-alikes'.
   actual, alley, apart, briefcase, can, chef, dome, fabric, human, lecture, massive, map, meaning, note, overhear, promotion.

Topic work

Working in groups draw up a list of as many different types of insurance as you can think of. Categorise them according to types of risk and decide which risks you think it most important to insure against.

2. Working for Lloyd's

A keen footballer and Arsenal supporter all through school, Mark was expecting to be put under contract to them as soon as he was old enough. When they rejected him, he wasn't willing to settle for second best and decided to leave school and get a job instead. Having concentrated on football, he did very badly in his exams and left Stepney Green School in July 1982 with an 'O' level in engineering.

He had no idea what he wanted to do although he was very confident he would get a job. He'd had three rejections when he saw an advertisement

Arsenal well-known football club in north London **to reject** refuse to accept **to settle for** accept **to do badly in** not be successful in **'O' level** GCE 'O' (Ordinary) level; examinations taken at school at the age of 16 **confident** with a belief in your own abilities on the board in the careers office offering trainee experience with a City firm. *It was a new scheme and the careers officer didn't know anything about it,* he remembers. *She asked me to come back afterwards if I got a place on it and tell her what I thought of the scheme.*

The interviewing process was comprehensive, an hour being asked general questions to see what sort of person you were, and a further 40 minutes outlining what was going to happen on the scheme. It was made clear that if you did well you could expect to get a job out of it. This was a good thing because *the duties as a trainee were really boring – photocopying, filing and general clerical duties. I only stuck it because I knew I would be able to move on to more interesting work and it gave you an opportunity to meet people and learn about the company.*

Mark started in September. By December, two jobs had come up for claims brokers on the North American side, one in aviation and one in non-marine. He accepted the job in non-marine and started in January. The job was to present claims to the underwriters. It was good experience for Mark to get to know where all the underwriters are at Lloyd's, and to get the general feel of the insurance market. After eight months, however, he decided he wanted to move on to the actual placing of insurance risks with underwriters. He was lucky that after just fourteen months he was offered the move.

The non-marine business is very broad, including everything from a string of racehorses to casualty insurance for the employees of a large company. Lloyd's has always specialised in the new and unusual. The latest is American embalmers trying to insure themselves against the risk of contracting AIDS. *I enjoy selling an insurance risk to an underwriter,* says Mark, *and it's so varied you learn something new every day.*

Usually, the minimum age to join Stewart Wrightson would be 19. By coming in as a trainee at 16, Mark is well up in his career. Although he

careers office office which helps young people find a job **trainee** s.o. who is being trained, especially in an office job **the City** financial area in central London **scheme** [ski:m] plan, programme **comprehensive** thorough **to outline** give the main details of **to file** G. ablegen **clerical** connected with office work **to stick s.th.** (coll.) continue to work hard at s.th. **to come up** G. frei werden **claims broker** G. Schadensprüfer **broker** s.o. who sells insurance **side** *here:* side of the business **aviation** *here:* insurance of aircraft **non-marine** *here:* insurance business not connected with shipping **claim** G. Anspruch **underwriter** G. Versicherungsgeber **to get the feel of s.th.** G. sich an etwas gewöhnen **to move on to** change to s.th. new or different **to place with** G. erteilen **a string of** *here:* line of **casualty** connected with being hurt or killed in an accident **embalmer** [ɪm'ba:mə] s.o. who treats a dead body with chemicals to stop it decaying **to contract** [kən'trækt] catch **Stewart Wrightson** an insurance broking company **to be well up** *here:* be making good progress knows he can do this job as well as anyone else and has the experience to prove it, he says it does leave him with a sense of insecurity not having the educational qualifications. In the next two to three years, his goal is to get some exams under his belt.

Deborah Arnolt (1985), *Getting to Know the Square Mile*. London: London Weekend Television. p. 15.

insecurity feeling of not being safe **goal** aim **under one's belt** (coll.) G. in seinem Besitz

Comprehension

What evidence is there in the passage that the following statements are true? If you don't think a statement is true explain what the passage really says.

1. Mark left school because he wasn't accepted as a football player by Arsenal.
2. Mark was confident he would get a job because he had one 'O' level.
3. During the interview Mark had to explain what he wanted to do in the training scheme.
4. It was not certain that all trainees would be given a job at the end of their traineeship.
5. Mark was more interested in meeting people than in doing office work.
6. Mark accepted the new job in non-marine insurance because he didn't want to move to North America.
7. Insurers at Lloyd's will now insure American embalmers against the risk of catching AIDS.
8. Mark has not been able to progress as quickly as he might have done if he had better educational qualifications.

Language skills

1. Look back at the text and find out which preposition follows the words and phrases listed below.
   put s.o. .... (contract)
   settle .... (second best)
   experience .... (a City firm)
   get a place .... (a training scheme)
   concentrate .... (football)
   specialise .... (the new and unusual)
   do well/badly .... (his exams)
   insure (yourself) .... (a risk)
2. Rewrite the following sentences without changing their meaning. Use the words and phrases from the exercise above and make any other necessary changes.
   1. Mark was accepted by the company for their training scheme.
   2. During his traineeship Mark only did clerical jobs such as photocopying and filing.

3. "Our insurance will cover damage to your house by flooding and storm."
4. I am not prepared to accept a job which means I have to do filing and photocopying all day long.
5. Mark was very successful in the tests he took at the interview.
6. After completing his traineeship he only dealt with non-marine insurance.
7. Because of the knowledge he had gained while working for Stewart Wrightson it would be easy for Mark to move to a better paid job in the City.
8. Looking back Mark wondered what would have happened if he had signed an agreement to play for Arsenal.

Topic work

1. One student should take the part of a reporter and the other the part of Mark Baptiste. Imagine Mark is being interviewed for a magazine aimed at young business people. Ask questions and give answers which will fill out and add background information to that given in the text.
   Discuss the results of your interviews afterwards. How similar or dissimilar are they?
2. a) Write a brief outline – as honestly as you can – of your personal characteristics in order to determine your suitability for a career. Think about a) your physical make-up, b) your aptitudes, c) what you have achieved and can achieve academically, d) your hobbies and leisure activities, and e) your personality and interests.
   b) Using the above points write a brief outline of Mark Baptiste's personal characteristics.
3. Compare Mark's job with that of the despatch riders in 'London's Lonesome Cowboys' (text II.1). Which of the jobs would you prefer and why?

3. A Brave New City

Half-past seven and the lanes of the City of London are astir with pedestrians picking their way to work through the misty light. All carry the same three objects: briefcase, *Financial Times* and paper coffee-cup with lid, with the occasional rolled umbrella.

Stock-market workers seldom see their spouses at breakfast. A number of City cafés serve breakfast, but the dedicated broker or equity salesman collects it from the canteen and eats it at his desk.

At 8 am the morning conference is held, when the firm's analysts, looking distinctly young, take turns at the microphone with the day's tips ... We're forecasting £220 million for the year so the price is not high ... Telecom, of course, it can only improve ... Oils: a lot of crude about ...

In the vast dealing room 200 people peer at their screens, which are arranged in banks along rows of desks, like an electronic classroom. The twilight glow of green display-text is broken by little blue and red blinks as prices are changed. The market-makers, who sit on a raised dais like monitors keeping order, are the youngest group because, like tennis players, they need to have lightning reactions. By now the telephones are busy with calls from managers of pension funds, insurance funds, unit trusts – the customers with millions to move.

Everyone is in shirt-sleeves – a nice class of shirt, though, as the salaries in this room range from about £50,000 for the experienced salesmen (and a few saleswomen) to more than £100,000 for the top few. Most of them are under 40, quite a

astir [ə'stɜ:] busy **pedestrian** s.o. travelling on foot **misty** foggy **briefcase** flat leather bag or case for carrying papers **Financial Times** financial newspaper **occasional** G. gelegentlich **stock market** G. Börse **spouse** husband or wife **dedicated** G. aufopfernd **broker** *here:* G. Börsenmakler **equity** G. Aktien **analyst** *here:* s.o. who analyses the financial markets **to take turns** G. miteinander wechseln **to forecast** say what is going to happen in the future **Telecom** British Telecom; large private company which runs Britain's telephone system **crude** crude oil; oil in its natural state **dealing room** room where shares are bought and sold **bank** many rows piled on top of each other forming a wall **twilight** the time when day is about to become night **display** what is shown on the screen **blink** going on and off **market-maker** s.o. who buys and sells shares for a client **dais** ['deɪɪs] raised part of the floor at one end of a room **monitor** a pupil whose job is to make sure other pupils behave **unit trust** a company through which you can buy a 'share' of shares in many different businesses few under 30. As a way of earning a lot of money young, stock-market trading has few rivals outside professional sport.

This is the New City. The scene that Big Bang has created is repeated all over the Square Mile as forced marriages are made between old comfortable-sized firms into vast conglomerates.

There was another City before Big Bang. Then the inhabitants operated from small, dingy offices and met on the Stock Exchange floor. There were the characters, nicknames, jokes and horseplay; everyone knew each other. 'My word is my bond' is a hard principle to dodge when you are dealing face to face. It's not quite the same when your deal on tape is your bond.

Today the busiest part of the Stock Exchange floor is the public gallery, where parties of schoolchildren and foreign visitors listen to a commentary and stare through windows at an empty space. It cost a fortune to install 20 years ago and now they're wondering what to do with it.

Yet just across Threadneedle Street is an aspect of the New City – the London Financial Futures Exchange (LIFFE) which explodes daily behind the classical portico of the old Royal Exchange building. From the public gallery here you look down on a sea of young men in brightly coloured blazers, which identify their firms, gesturing and shouting like a school sports day that has turned into a free-for-all. They are trading financial 'futures' – a way of insuring against heavy losses on deals to be settled later, through future changes in the exchange rates, or in the Stock Exchange index.

Brian Williamson, the chairman of LIFFE (known simply as 'Life'),

rival s.o. with whom you compete **professional** done by people who are paid **Big Bang** changes made to the running of London's stock exchange (Börse) in October 1986 **the Square Mile** another name for the City **conglomerate** a large business organisation consisting of different companies that produce goods of different kinds **dingy** ['dɪndʒɪ] dirty **character** a strange or humorous person **nickname** a name used instead of s.o.'s own name **horseplay** G. Balgerei **My word is my bond** the motto of the Stock Exchange: My word can be trusted **to dodge** avoid **deal** G. Geschäft, Handel **Threadneedle Street** street in the City famous for its banks, including the Bank of England **LIFFE** [laɪf] London International Financial Futures Exchange; a market where 'futures', i.e. contracts to buy or sell money at some time in the future can be bought or sold **portico** G. Portikus **Royal Exchange** opened in 1844 by Queen Victoria, home of LIFFE since 1982 **blazer** ['bleɪzə] a jacket, often with a school or club sign on the top pocket **gesture** ['dʒestʃə] **free-for-all** G. Gerangel **to trade** buy and sell **futures** contracts to buy or sell money or goods at some time in the future **exchange rate** the value of money from one country compared to that of another country **index** list showing the prices of shares explains that, 'what Lloyd's is to the householder or car-owner, we are to the financial institutions'.

Seats on the exchange are so sought after that they change hands for £200,000. It has brought forth a new breed of trader – tough, leather-lunged, hard-living, hard-swearing, surviving by the swiftness of his calculations and gut-reactions. Many are East-Enders. Some picked up their early experience in street markets and one even used to shine shoes outside until he was invited in by one of his customers. The rest of the City calls them 'barrow boys', while they refer to the blue-blooded Oxbridge stockbrokers as 'spoons' (silver-spoon-in-the-mouth).

There is a champagne bar outside the dealers' entrance to the exchange but most of these traders prefer to drink beer from the can at the nearby Cock and Woolpack. Nothing could better illustrate the tale of two Cities.

Lunchtime conversation in the Woolpack confirms this. 'We're the New City,' said one young man in a brilliant red blazer. 'Doesn't matter to us who you are or where you come from, so long as you're good.' 'There are no "nice guys" on that floor,' said another in colourful checks. 'I prefer to work with people I can trust. About as far as I can throw them.'

A member of the floor supervising staff explains that fortunes can be made here. 'I could name three who have made a million. They're still trading. We've had a fist fight or two. We step in if we see something starting and they can be fined up to £100.'

Most of them are in their 20s and are employed by banks and securities houses at salaries upwards of £40,000. A few deal on their own account with their own money.

The Mail on Sunday,
'You' Magazine, date not known.

Lloyd's market where insurance is bought and sold **to change hands** G. den Besitzer wechseln **to bring forth** produce **breed** type, kind **trader** s.o. who buys and sells **tough** G. zäh **hard-living** living a life full of difficulties, problems and work **hard-swearing** using a lot of swear-words **gut-reaction** G. rein gefühlsmäßige Reaktion **East-Ender** from the East-End, therefore of working-class origin **to pick up** gain, obtain **barrow boy** man or boy who sells goods from a cart **blue-blooded** aristocratic **Oxbridge** describing s.o. who studied at Oxford or Cambridge University **stockbroker** G. Börsenmakler **Cock, Woolpack** names of public houses **guy** (coll.) man **to supervise** ['su:pəvaɪz] **to step in** G. einschreiten **securities house** firm which buys and sells stocks and shares (Wertpapiere) **upwards of** more than **on their own account** for their own advantage

Comprehension

1. What, briefly, are the differences between the 'old' and the 'new' City?
2. What impression does the writer give of the people who work in the City? Look at his comments on their age, what they earn, their social class, and their attitudes.

Language skills

1. Find words and phrases in the passage which mean the same as the definitions below:
   a) walk carefully
   b) place where a worker in a factory or office can eat
   c) look at carefully
   d) sum of money used to pay people when they are too old to work
   e) firms have to join together
   f) large sum of money
   g) making signs with their arms and hands
   h) someone who owns a house
   i) wanted very much
   j) who watch other people work
   k) made to pay money in order to punish them
2. In the following parts of the passage the writer expresses ideas indirectly – and therefore in some cases humorously – rather than stating them directly. Write down briefly what you think he means by the following sentences and phrases.
   a) 'Stock-market workers seldom see their spouses at breakfast.' (l. 9/10)
   b) '... the dedicated broker collects [his breakfast] from the canteen and eats it at his desk.' (l. 12–14)
   c) '... the firm's analysts, looking distinctly young ...' (l. 16/17)
   d) '... the customers with millions to move.' (l. 38/39)
   e) 'Everyone is in shirt-sleeves – a nice class of shirt, though, ...' (l. 40/41)
   f) ''My word is my bond' is a hard principle to dodge when you are dealing face to face. It's not quite the same when your deal on tape is your bond.' (l. 63–67).
   g) 'It cost a fortune to install 20 years ago and now they're wondering what to do with it.' (l. 73–76)
   h) '... Nothing could better illustrate the tale of two Cities.' (l. 122/123)
   i) "Doesn't matter who you are or where you come from, so long as you're good." (l. 127–129)
   j) "I prefer to work with people I can trust. About as far as I can throw them." (l. 132–134)

Topic work

1. Use this text as the basis for a project on the City of London. This could be carried out in groups with each group finding out about one City institution: Lloyd's, the Stock Exchange, LIFFE, the Bank of England, and others not mentioned here, such as the Commodity markets, the Livery Companies, the merchant and clearing banks, and the political organisation of the City under its Lord Mayor and Corporation.
2. Form two groups. One group should prepare the case for the motion: "Greed for money is the root of all evil" and the other should prepare the case for the motion: "Money makes the world go round."

4. The City – a poem

The City

Business men with awkward hips
And dirty jokes upon their lips,
And large behinds and jingling chains,
And riddled teeth and riddling brains,
And plump white fingers made to curl
Round some anaemic city girl,
And so lend colour to the lives
And old suspicions of their wives.

Young men who wear on office stools
The ties of minor public schools,
Each learning how to be a sinner
And tell 'a good one' after dinner,
And so discover it is rather
Fun to go one more than father.
But father, son and clerk join up
To talk about the Football Cup.

John Betjeman (1932)

awkward ['ɔ:kwəd] G. schwerfällig **hip** G. Hüfte **behind** G. Hintern **jingling** ['dʒɪŋglɪŋ] G. Klimpern **riddled** full of holes **to riddle** G. rätseln **plump** fat **anaemic** *here:* pale and weak **to lend** *here:* give **stool** seat without back or arms **minor** *here:* unimportant, not well-known **public school** private school **'a good one'** *here:* a good joke **to go one more than** go further than **clerk** [kla:k] s.o. who does general office work **to join up** *here:* meet

Topic work

1. Summarise briefly the theme of the poem.
2. Explain the effect of the following words and phrases:
   - 'jingling chains'
   - 'riddling brains'
   - '. . . lend colour to the lives/And old suspicions of their wives.'

3. Characterise the men presented in the text.
   What is the writer's attitude towards them?
   Does the writer present a fair picture?
4. Identify the formal elements which hold the poem together and give it a sense of continuity.

5. London: No Place to Hide

You would think this would be a great time to be a tourist in London. After all, with the pound still quite weak, a visitor with foreign currency to spend should be able to live in style, make the scene, indulge his fondest fantasies, right? You could start off, say, by going to Savile Row to have a suit made by the celebrated street's most celebrated tailor, Huntsman. Then nip over to Jermyn Street to order a dozen candy-striped shirts from Turnbull & Asser. Later on, dinner at Le Gavroche (arguably, the finest French restaurant in town), and finally to the theater to take in London's hottest musical, "Starlight Express".

Guess again.

Not to put too fine a point on it, London this summer has been overrun by a horde of foreigners the likes of which hasn't been seen since the Roman legions pulled up stakes and went home 1,600 years ago. One is tempted to compare the crowds that jam Piccadilly at lunchtime these days to the massed and twisted bodies that fill Michelangelo's great vision of the damned on the end wall of the Sis-

to indulge one's fantasies G. seinen Fantasien nachgeben **fond** dear **Savile Row** ['sævɪl rəʊ] street in the West End where many famous and expensive tailors can be found **to nip over to** (coll.) go quickly for a short time **Jermyn Street** ['dʒɜ:mɪn] street in the West End where there are many shirtmakers **candy-striped** having narrow coloured lines on a white background **arguably** there are arguments for saying **theater** (American spelling) **to take in** *here:* see **not to put too fine a point on it** express it clearly, plainly **the likes of which** of a kind which **legion** ['li:dʒən] a division of an army **to pull up stakes** (coll.) *here:* leave, go away **to jam** gather in a small place **these days** nowadays **massed** crowded **twisted** bent into strange shapes **Michelangelo** [ˌmaɪkəl'ændʒələʊ] Michelangelo Buonarroti (1475–1564); poet, sculptor, painter, architect from Florence

Lining up to watch the changing of the guard at Buckingham Palace: A welcome influx of dollars, lire, marks, dinars and francs (*Woodfin Camp,* New York)

tine Chapel. But, then, none of Michelangelo's condemned are wearing backpacks. In all, nearly 9 million foreign visitors are expected to stream through the greater London area this year. And while shopkeepers are understandably delighted by the resulting influx of dollars, lire, marks, dinars and francs, less fortunate locals are starting to understand what the Australian aborigines must have felt like when the white men began pouring into Botany Bay. . . .

Humble commuters, too, are feeling the tourist heel on their necks. Catching a tube train or double-decker bus has become almost impossible, so clogged are they with gigantic Australian, American and Scandinavian teenagers bowed under backpacks and bedrolls the size of telephone booths. Entrances to the underground are particularly difficult to negotiate, it apparently being the custom of these visitors to wait until they reach the portals before stopping to unfold large maps of the city to find out where they are.

For resident Londoners quite understandably driven to seek peace and quiet and spiritual nourishment away from the seething

Sistine Chapel the chapel in the Vatican at Rome; decorated with frescoes by Michelangelo **condemned** *here:* G. die Verdammten **in all** as the total **fortunate** G. vom Glück begünstigt **aborigine** [ˌæbəˈrɪdʒənɪ] s.o. who lived in Australia before the Europeans came **Botany Bay** place near Sydney where the British founded the first colony in Australia **humble** G. bescheiden **commuter** s.o. who regularly travels a long distance between home and work **bowed** [baʊd] bent **bedroll** roll of bedding for sleeping in a tent **portal** gate, entrance **resident** s.o. who lives in the place **nourishment** [ˈnʌrɪʃmənt] G. Nahrung **seething** G. drängend mass, it is no comfort to step into the vaulted cool of Westminster Abbey – not when one is likely to be trampled at any minute by 50 Germans seeking the tombs of Henry VII and Elizabeth I. Nor is there any refuge to be found these days in the normally silent National Gallery. Try to concentrate your thoughts on a favorite masterpiece – say the "Wilton Diptych," painted in about 1395 when the only tourists were Flemish weavers – and your reverie will invariably be shattered by a loud, female American voice shrieking, "Look, George, the Wilton Triptych. It's very old."

No relief in sight: Shoved, pushed, starved, deprived of decent bespoke clothing – the average Londoner cannot even console himself with the knowledge that soon the invaders will have gone. The figures show they now stay longer, and that every year there are more of them. In 1974 a mere 8.5 million visitors came to the whole of Britain. By 1984 the number had climbed to almost 14 million; this year will bring a million more than that.

In a parliamentary debate on tourism late last year, a less than enthusiastic Tory M.P. quoted the text of a new prayer promulgated by the Orthodox Church in Greece asking the Lord to have mercy on Greek cities and islands "which are scourged by the world touristic wave" and asking protection "from these contemporary Western invaders." But alas, the M.P. was a voice in the wilderness, drowned out by a chorus of reminders that tourism now earns Britain more foreign currency – an estimated $ 6.5 billion this year alone – than any other industry except oil.

Given the importance of tourism to Britain's ailing economy, it's hardly surprising that Sunday Times columnist John Huxley took it upon himself last month to pub-

comfort G. Trost **vaulted** ['vɔːltɪd] G. gewölbt **Westminster Abbey** church where almost all English kings and queens since William I have been crowned **to trample** G. treten **National Gallery** located on the north side of Trafalgar Square; contains over 2000 European paintings **favorite** (American spelling) **Wilton Diptych** ['dɪptɪk] a painting on two pieces of wood joined together **Flemish** coming from the region of Flanders **reverie** thoughts **to shatter** *here:* disturb suddenly **to shove** [ʃʌv] push in a violent way **to deprive s.o. of** stop s.o. getting or having **bespoke** specially made to s.o.'s measurements **to console oneself** G. sich trösten **mere** [mɪə] bloß **Tory** Conservative **to promulgate** ['prɒməlgeɪt] G. verkünden **the Lord** God **to scourge** [skɜːdʒ] G. geißeln **alas** (arch.) [əl'æs] *here:* G. leider **drowned out by** *here:* G. überschwemmt durch **reminder** *here:* words that make you remember s.th. **billion** thousand million **given that** *here:* if we accept that **to take it upon o.s. to do s.th.** G. meinen, man müsse etwas tun licly scold what he described as the country's "surly taxi drivers, sloppy hotel and restaurant staff, dozy tourism officials..." But perhaps these folk should be considered the noble defenders of Britain's insular attitudes, deserving of praise from a grateful nation. For it may be that only traditional bloody-mindedness, loathing of things and people foreign, and good old British idleness will preserved some remnant of a once-great nation's character.

Tony Clifton, *Newsweek,* August 19, 1985.

to scold G. ausschimpfen **surly** G. mürrisch **sloppy** G. schlampig **dozy** ['dəʊzɪ] G. dösig **folk** [fəʊk] people **insular** ['ɪnsju:lə] island **bloody-mindedness** [ˌblʌdi'maɪndɪdnɪs] (coll.) G. Sturheit **loathing** ['ləʊðɪŋ] strong dislike, hatred **idleness** laziness

Comprehension

Write brief notes on:

1. the problems tourists cause to London and Londoners;
2. the advantages gained from having tourists in London;
3. the people who suffer most from the tourists in London;
4. the people who gain from having tourists in London.

Language skills

The writer uses a number of expressions which make his style interesting but a little difficult to understand. What does he mean by the following phrases?

a) '...locals are starting to understand what the Australian aborigines must have felt like when the white men began pouring into Botany Bay.' (l. 42–46)
b) '...commuters are feeling the tourist heel on their necks.' (l. 47–49)
c) '...your reverie will invariably be shattered by...' (l. 80/81)
d) '...the average Londoner cannot even console himself with the knowledge that soon the invader will have gone.' (l. 87–90)
e) '... the M.P. was a voice in the wilderness, drowned out by a chorus of reminders...' (l. 109–111)
f) '... these folk should be considered the noble defenders of Britain's insular attitudes...' (l. 125–127)

Topic work

1. How are a) the tourists and b) Londoners and the British characterised in the article? The writer creates a humorous effect by using exaggerated comparisons and metaphors. Find examples of these aspects of the writer's style and explain their humour.
2. Work in groups of three or four, some groups taking the part of tourists who have visited London, some groups taking the part of Londoners. The tourists should write letters complaining about the conditions and service they faced in London and the Londoners should write letters in which they express their annoyance at the behaviour of tourists in their city. Read out the letters and discuss in class.
3. Tourism: blessing or blight? Discuss.

6. Capital Radio 95.8

Capital Facts

Capital Radio – London's music station playing 24 hours a day in stereo – went on the air at 5 am on October 16th 1973, with an announcement from chairman, Richard Attenborough, now Sir Richard. The first record played on air was Bridge Over Troubled Water and the first commercial was for fish fingers.

The Independent Broadcasting Authority granted Capital the franchise for London's general and entertainment station (while giving LBC the franchise for news and information) in 1973 and in October 1983 it was extended to 1992.

The last survey of Capital Radio showed that Capital had an audience of 3,171,000 a week. (This figure is estimated to rise to over 4m) The survey, published in the Spring 1987 shows that each listener tunes in for an average of 10 hours 18 minutes a week. Capital's listeners tune in to the station a total of 29m hours a week.

to go on the air broadcast programmes **announcement** public statement **chairman** s.o. who directs the work of a committee or organisation **Sir Richard Attenborough** ['ætənbrə] former actor, now film producer and director **Independent Broadcasting Authority** G. Behörde, die das private Rundfunkwesen beaufsichtigt **to grant** give **franchise** ['fræntʃaɪz] special right given to a company to operate in a certain area **LBC** London Broadcasting Company **survey** G. Umfrage **to tune in** set your radio to receive broadcasts from a certain station

There are about 140 members of staff from Managing Director to post boy, plus a number of freelance staff on contract. The programmes are, of course, the heart of the station and the programme department is the biggest. Not only are there more than 24 DJs and presenters to keep the station on air 24 hours a day, seven days a week, but there are back-up staff. Their duties range from producing programmes to secretarial tasks, compiling traffic news and keeping careful note of every record played. (Royalties have to be paid to various organisations such as the Performing Rights Society and Phonographic Performance Ltd.) Broadly speaking, the programme department is divided into two. One part deals with music (the compilation of the playlist is a weekly task of mammoth proportions, for in an average week there are as many as 100 new singles, all of which have to be heard before the list can be made up.) The other deals with the spoken word, producing Capital Reports (the news features which go out three times each weekday), and The Way It Is at 7 pm each weekday evening.

Actual news bulletins are taken on the hour from Independent Radio News, an adjunct of LBC, the other independent London local radio station which complements, rather than competes with, Capital. (See earlier reference.)

One of the better known services which Capital provides off the air is Helpline, the advice, information and referral service which is conducted confidentially on the telephone and took 32,224 calls in 1986. But under the head of community affairs there are others – the Jobfinder for the young unemployed and the Flatshare lists which are given out at 11 am on Tuesdays and printed in the NME (New Musical Express), and which contain details of rooms and shares all over London compiled from information phoned in by Capital listeners.

Managing Director the head of a company **post boy** s.o. who takes letters and parcels to the post office **freelance** s.o. who earns their money without being in the regular employment of any particular organisation **staff** people who work for a company, usually in an office **DJ** disc jockey **presenter** s.o. who presents a radio show **back-up** supporting, helping **secretarial** work connected with being a secretary; writing letters, arranging meetings **to compile** [kəm'paɪl] *here:* collect and write down information **to keep note of** write down **royalties** G. Tantiemen **broadly speaking** in general **compilation** [ˌkɒmpɪ'leɪʃn] G. Zusammenstellung **playlist** list of records to be played **mammoth** ['mæməθ] very large **feature** report **actual** G. eigentlich **bulletin** ['bʊlɪtɪn] a short report **on the hour** at 1 o'clock, 2 o'clock... exactly **adjunct** ['ædʒʌŋkt] *here:* G. Tochterfirma **to complement** ['kɒmplɪmənt] G. ergänzen **referral** [rɪ'fɜːrəl] h. a service which tells people where they can find special help **to conduct** G. betreiben **confidentially** [ˌkɒnfɪ'denʃlɪ] **shares** flats you can live in with other people, each paying a part of the rent

The main source of Capital's income is the air time we sell to advertisers. Unlike the BBC we are not financed by the licence fee. Thus, the sales department provides the lifeblood of the organisation. (Capital merchandise – T shirts, pencil souvenirs, key rings, umbrellas etc. – on sale in the foyer account for only a tiny proportion of income.)

The IBA lays down that there can be nine minutes of commercials in any one hour (compared with television's seven). There are also rules about who may advertise on the air and about the form in which these advertisements may appear. (The IBA, 70 Brompton Road, London SW3, supplies copies of the advertising regulations.)

Capital Radio Limited, Euston Tower, London NW1 3DR.

air time broadcasting time **advertiser** s.o. who puts an advertisement in a newspaper, on radio, or on TV **fee** money you pay for a service **merchandise** goods to be sold **foyer** ['fɔɪeɪ] entrance hall of a large building; here of Capital Radio's head office at Euston Tower **to lay down** G. festlegen **commercial** advertisement on radio or TV **rule** G. Vorschrift

Comprehension

After carefully reading the passage say which of the following statements are true or false according to the text?

1. The number of listeners to Capital Radio is falling.
2. More than 29 million people listen to Capital Radio every week.
3. Each listener listens to Capital Radio for more than 10 hours a week.
4. Disc jockeys have to keep a note of each record played.
5. Most staff at Capital Radio work for one of two main departments.
6. All records played on Capital Radio are heard before being played.
7. Capital Radio staff have nothing to do with the hourly news bulletins.
8. Helpline broadcasts details of places and people where you can get information and advice.
9. The NME publishes details of the flats and jobs which are broadcast on Capital Radio.
10. The sales department organises the sale of T shirts and other merchandise in the foyer of Euston Tower.
11. There is more advertising allowed on radio than on television.

Language skills

Advice and information are words which are always singular in English, but are usually plural in German. Using a grammar book and dictionary look up other words which are singular in English and plural in German.
There are also words which are plural in English (i. e. have a plural form and take a plural verb) but singular in German, e. g. instructions vs. Anleitung. Using a grammar book find as many of these words with their German equivalent as you can.

Topic work

1. Name the jobs mentioned in the passage. Which one would you like to have and why? Which one would you not like to have? Why not?
2. Produce a radio programme in English about your town which would be useful and interesting for English-speaking visitors. This can be done in groups and recorded on cassette. Finally, compare the programmes produced by the different groups.
3. The students are the members of a committee who have to decide whether to allow a commercial radio station to be set up in their area. Form two groups: those who are for the proposal and those who are against. Each side should prepare its case and hold a meeting with a final vote.

A LONDON CHRONOLOGY

43	The second Roman invasion of Britain during the reign of Emperor Claudius, the Romans build London bridge and establish a garrison at Londinium.
60–61	Queen Boadicea leads her tribe against the Romans, burns down Londinium; the Romans rebuild the town.
200	The Romans build a defensive wall around London with seven gates; London's population is about 50000.
410	The Romans withdraw their troops from London.
467	The Saxon invasion of England.
604	According to the chronicler Bede, the first St Paul's Cathedral is built.
842	The Vikings attack London.
886	King Alfred defeats the Viking Danes and establishes London as a market town.
1052	Edward the Confessor makes London his capital.
1066	After defeating Harold, William the Conqueror defeats London and is crowned at Westminster Abbey.
1070s	William I starts to build the White Tower of the Tower of London as a defence against the London mob.
1176	London Bridge, the only bridge across the Thames until 1739, is built.
1191	Richard I recognises the City of London as a self-governing community.
1192	Henry Fitz Elwin becomes the first mayor of London.
1280	Old St Paul's Cathedral is completed.
1348–50	The Black Death.
1411–40	Guildhall, the administrative centre of the City, is built.
1477	William Caxton publishes the first book printed in Britain, printed on his press at Westminster.
1566	The Royal Exchange is founded, which enables London to compete with Amsterdam in trading.
1599	The Globe Theatre is built.
1605	The Gunpowder Plot – Guy Fawkes and conspirators try to blow up Parliament and the royal family.

1637 Charles I opens London's first public royal park.
1665 The Great Plague kills almost 100,000 people.
1666 The Great Fire begins on Sept 2 in Pudding Lane and destroys fourfifths of the City.
1670 Christopher Wren starts designing his 51 City churches, including St Paul's Cathedral (1675–1711).
1680s Lloyd's marine insurance market is founded in Edward Lloyd's coffee house.
1694 The Bank of England is founded.
1739 London's second bridge, Westminster Bridge is opened.
1759 The British Museum is opened.
1762 George III moves into Buckingham Palace, which becomes the official royal residence.
1801 The first population census: 959,000.
1802 The Stock Exchange is founded.
London is the largest port in the world.
1824 National Gallery is founded.
1826 University College, the earliest part of the University of London, is founded.
1829 A horse-drawn bus service begins along Marylebone Road.
Sir Robert Peel establishes the Metropolitan Police.
1830 London Zoo opens.
1834 Palace of Westminster burns down: rebuilt 1835–60.
1837 Queen Victoria, aged 18, is crowned.
Euston, the first main line rail terminus, is built.
1841 Royal Botanical Gardens at Kew opens to the public.
1843 The world's first underwater pedestrian tunnel opens, Rotherhithe-Wapping.
1847 Following the Great Potato Famine 100,000 Irish arrive and form 20% of London's population.
1851 Population: 2.3m. The Great Exhibition is held in Hyde Park.
1860 Victoria Station opens.
1863 Metropolitan Railway opens, the world's first urban underground train service.
1870 London's first tramcar service.
1880s Many Jews arrive, fleeing anti-semitic pogroms in Poland and Russia.
1884–89 London's first deluxe hotel, the Savoy, is built, followed by the Ritz (1906) and the Dorchester (1928–31).
1888 London County Council is established to govern 117 square miles of London, except the City.

1890	The first tube runs with electric trains.
1897	Tate Gallery opens.
1901	Building starts on Harrods in Knightsbridge, followed by Selfridges (1907).
1901	Population of Greater London: 6.5m. Queen Victoria dies.
1922	First daily radio programmes from Savoy Hill.
1927	BBC established.
1936	Television broadcasting begins from Alexandra Palace.
1939–45	Second World War.
1940–41	(Sep.–May) The Blitz.
1940s	London's population reaches peak of about 10m.
1950s	Start of immigration from West Indies and Asian subcontinent.
1951	Population of Greater London: 8.2m. Festival of Britain held on South Bank of the Thames.
1952	Queen Elizabeth succeeds to the throne.
1956	Clean Air Act puts an end to London smog.
1965	Greater London Council is established to run London, replaces London County Council.
1974	Covent Garden fruit and vegetable market moves outside central London to Nine Elms; local people save, restore and revive the old market buildings.
1976	National Theatre complex opens; Museum of London opens.
1977	Underground line to Heathrow Airport opens.
1981	London Docklands Development Corporation (LDDC) is established to redevelop the 400 acres of redundant London docks. The NatWest Tower, 600 feet tall, London's tallest building, is opened.
1982	The Thames Barrier, designed to protect London from flooding, is opened.
1986	Population of Greater London: 6.7m; Parliament abolishes the Greater London Council.
1987	Opening of the Dockland's light railway and London City Airport.
1990	Abolition of the Inner London Education Authority.
1991	Opening of Canary Wharf, Europe's largest office development.

987 654 321